Just Carry On Breathing: A Year Surviving Suicide and Widowhood

Gary Marson

An imprint of Bennion Kearny

Published in 2016 by Dark River, an imprint of Bennion Kearny Limited.

Copyright © Dark River 2016

ISBN: 978-1-911121-08-4

Published by Dark River, an imprint of Bennion Kearny Limited
6 Woodside
Churnet View Road
Oakamoor
ST10 3AE

For my beautiful wife Louise.

This is the book that I wish with all my heart and soul I never had to write.

My love for you is eternal. I miss you so very much.

All the author's royalties will be donated to the Louise Tebboth Foundation and WAY Widowed and Young.

The Louise Tebboth Foundation, established in memory of Gary's wife, aims to provide financial assistance to projects and services which support the mental well-being of doctors in England and Wales and initiatives assisting the bereaved families of doctors who have died by suicide. Further information can be found at *www.louisetebboth.org.uk*

WAY Widowed and Young is the only national charity in the UK for men and women aged 50 or under when their partner died. Founded in 1997, WAY now has more than 2,000 members across England, Wales, Scotland and Northern Ireland. The charity provides peer-to-peer support to young widowed men and women – married or not, with or without children, whatever their sexual orientation – as they adjust to life after the death of their partner. Find out more at the website *www.widowedandyoung.org.uk*

In the Beginning There Was the End

It's the easiest of all telephone numbers to remember, one that is drummed into each of us from childhood. Newspapers regularly feature toddlers who manage to use it to call for emergency assistance. But in my panic and shock I couldn't get it right. 999. Just one digit to press three times, yet somehow it took my trembling hands several attempts to make the connection.

My entire world had collapsed seconds previously. Working late on a Friday evening, concentrating on meeting the deadline for completion of the most critical task of the year, it had taken me some time to realise that my latest texts to Louise had gone unanswered. I was so distracted that, at first, I found nothing odd in her failure to respond to my subsequent phone calls, despite such silence being highly unusual. We were *always* in close contact with each other.

Realisation crept upon me slowly at first. A hideous, unthinkable, explanation began to gradually form in my mind, growing in intensity and urgency. More telephone calls were made and messages left, the words still measured but the tone increasingly concerned. Almost as if paralysed by the immensity of my thoughts, bizarrely I continued to work for a few minutes until suddenly, in an instant, I knew. Louise had attempted to take her life and was probably dead.

As I hurried down the wide, imposing staircase out of my offices and sped through the dark, mercifully traffic-free, streets on the short drive home, I was already entering the bubble of unreality that would surround me for months to come, my mind and body almost split in two, as if I was observing somebody else. I still tried to cling, but with little conviction, to the explanation of a fault with Louise's notoriously unreliable cheap mobile phone. I told myself that I would know as soon as I saw the house. As soon as I saw whether the light coming from the windows suggested normal occupation.

It didn't. The downstairs of the house was in darkness but our bedroom light was blazing, with the curtains wide open. Louise would never have left it like that, nor could she have fallen asleep in those conditions.

A silent extended scream of pain, despair and rage was already beginning to form in the pit of my stomach and extend to every fibre of my body. And then I saw the note taped to the front door: 'Gary, please don't come in on your own. Call 999 first. I'm so sorry. Louise'. It was timed at 5pm. It was now 8.45pm. I was far too late.

I now knew not only that Louise was almost certainly dead but also the method she had used. I knew that I would find her in the hallway. Despite her warning I had to try to get to her, just in case. But the front door was locked from the inside. When I finally managed to get through to the emergency services, the operator put me on hold, seeking advice from a supervisor because of the warning not to enter the house. I couldn't wait for them to get back to me.

In my panic I completely forgot that there is a side access to the back garden and ran instead to the alley behind the house, frantically trying to kick down the fence panels before my befuddled brain recalled the easier route. I made my way through the blackness of the garden and wasn't surprised to find the conservatory doors were unlocked, deliberately left open by Louise to provide for this alternative access.

It's just a few short paces from the back door into the kitchen and from there I knew that I would be able to see straight through into the hallway. I was braced for the sight in front of me. My beautiful wife, hanging from the bannisters.

I was drawn by some strange inner force to walk through the darkened kitchen towards Louise. I stood in front of her, looking up into her wide open eyes. Her head was bowed, her face battleship grey. It was the first time that I had ever seen a dead body. By now the emergency services were back on the line to me. Could I cut her down? I was afraid of touching her, feeling her cold body. I was afraid of her crumpling in a heap on the floor. I was afraid of everything that was to come. I was instructed to get out of the house. I stumbled in a daze onto the road and waited, listening to the emergency sirens which I could already hear fast approaching.

It was Friday 23rd January 2015. Louise was just 40 years of age.

*

It never occurred to me that I might be the one left behind. It wasn't a possibility that we ever spoke about or I was prepared for. Louise was nearly six years younger than me, physically fitter and lived a much healthier lifestyle. My assumption, insofar as I ever thought about the subject, was that it would be her who would – at some point in the remote future – face the prospect of widowhood. Not me. And certainly not now.

We met relatively late in life, through an online dating service, in June 2010 and were married in September 2011. Louise was 36 and I was 43. Neither of us brought much prior experience of relationships and ours had very much the feel of a younger love, with the excitement, novelty, exploration and intensity of teenage sweethearts. Both of us visibly blossomed. After waiting so long this, finally, was our time.

We complemented each other perfectly. Where one was weak the other was strong. We shared common values and approaches to life and enjoyed a gentle and mutually supportive relationship, one in which we each spent all our time looking after the needs of the other. Neither of us were comfortable with confrontation or anger and although there were inevitably sometimes difficult conversations we never once had an argument. We did almost everything as a couple, taking a delight in actively sharing in each other's interests.

I could never quite believe my luck in finding Louise. She was the kindest, most gentle, wise and humble person I have ever met. A gifted doctor working in general practice in a socially-deprived area of South East London, she cared passionately about people and making their lives better, instinctively supporting the underdog and seeing beauty and goodness in those where others saw none. She was much loved by her colleagues for her intelligence, commitment, energy, enthusiasm and sense of fun. She was also hugely popular with her patients, giving unreservedly to provide them with the best possible care, often at the expense of her own wellbeing. The phrase they used time and again was 'the best doctor I ever had'.

Louise was also a talented painter, and loved the arts, cycling, running and birdwatching. She was never happier than when she was outdoors, close to the nature that so enchanted her. A much-adored Aunt and almost equally loved by her numerous godchildren, she was increasingly politically active in an effort to maintain the values and services of the National Health Service to which she was so committed. Her energy, enthusiasm and zest for life left most people trailing in her wake.

But there was a shadow over Louise's life, and our relationship. She fought a long battle with extraordinary strength, determination and tenacity against intermittent but insidious depression arising from what had been diagnosed as bipolar disorder. Louise constantly attempted to analyse and understand what she often described as her 'full head' and sometimes challenged the precise nature of the diagnosis. But whatever the description, the impact and outcome was the same. At intervals, Louise was gripped with anxiety and struggled to find either energy or hope. She was fortunate to survive what should have been a fatal overdose in her late twenties.

We knew the pattern and recognised the signs, extended periods of buoyancy punctuated by acute crises of confidence and direction. Distressing and unsettling though the periods of illness were there was, however, always comfort in the certainty of rapid recovery. The overdose was a long time in the past. However difficult things got, there had been no suggestion a repeat was likely. It was easy for me, with no personal memory of the experience, to dismiss its continuing relevance. In any case, who could possibly imagine their wife ending her own life?

So I was initially slow to spot the potential danger as Louise struggled with an exceptionally deep and prolonged episode of depression in the second half of 2014. This time, whenever she seemed to be on the verge of recovery, something happened to plunge her back into darkness. Most notably, days after we returned from an uplifting holiday to Sicily, just as Louise seemed close to a return to work and normality, her father took his life. We found ourselves in the midst of very similar scenes to those that I would witness again, even closer to home, three months later.

But Louise continued to fight and against the odds we enjoyed a hopeful, if gentle, Christmas, with recovery once more apparently in sight. An appointment with her psychiatrist in the New Year provided her with an opportunity to press for an earlier-than-planned return to her beloved job, the role from which she took so much satisfaction and meaning.

I watched her closely as the psychiatrist gave the same advice I had the previous evening; be gentle on yourself, wait another couple of weeks. The light which had been shining brightly in her eyes went out instantly. It never came back on again. The wait was more than she could bear. Within a week Louise was admitting to me a plan to overdose. Despite the intervention of psychiatric services, daily monitoring and our planning of an intensive regime of activity to keep her occupied and safe, the end came ten days later.

Nothing can prepare you for loss of this magnitude, and in this way. In the last desperate weeks, I had begun to accept the theoretical risk, to allow for the possibility that it might, someday, be our experience. Having seen at close quarters the immediate aftermath of my father-in-law's death I was even able to visualise events, with, as it turned out, almost uncanny accuracy. But none of this helps absorb the shock or allows easy acceptance of the reality. It is simply too enormous. The last year has not been a life that I recognise as my own.

But if anything has enabled me to at least attempt to adjust to the new realities of my life as a widower, to process my response to the destruction of my world and to make sense of suicide, then it is writing, initially in my diary, then on my blog, from which many of the chapters in these pages are drawn, and subsequently in this book. I found the discipline required to do it calming. At my lowest points, I would invariably reach for my laptop and type through the tears until the eye of the storm had passed. It has allowed me to better understand my grief and connected me with so many others walking a similar path.

Inevitably, the sharing of my story has also required aspects of Louise's to be told too. They are two sides of the same coin, diverging only at the moment of her death. I have never been in any doubt that Louise would wholeheartedly approve. She never sought to hide or deny the challenges that she faced and her desire to use her father's death as an opportunity to fully disclose these to family and friends, and thereby promote understanding of mental illness, provided me with something of a template for the way in which I believe she would want me to respond to her own.

I hope that in doing so I am making her proud of me. I do not have Louise's professional skills, knowledge and experience to make a difference in this world. But I do have the power of our story and I will use it here and wherever I can to enable Louise to continue, indirectly, to reach out to help people even now, just as she would want.

I cannot do this by writing a self-help manual in order to assist those who have lost their partners take a shortcut through the worst of the pain they will experience. There is no one way in which we should mourn. Although the emotions we encounter on the journey are almost universal, our responses to them are uniquely individual. Everybody finds their own way through, and must do so alone. Nobody can ease this burden for us, however difficult that may be for family and friends to come to terms with.

Nevertheless, I know how closely I watched others some months further down this path than myself. I was desperately looking for reassurance that I was not the only one making the journey, that the maelstrom of confusing and often contradictory thoughts, worries and emotions that swirled constantly around me were normal that my tears, fatigue, loneliness and, sometimes, my curious ability to continue with life, did not make me a freak.

And I was also looking for hope, signs that the journey could be survived and a new, happy and fulfilling life subsequently established. One that was inevitably different, but still good. I was scared that at 46 the short period of happiness which it had taken me so long to find, and which had been so quickly and cruelly snatched away from me, was as good as it got. I feared that the rest of my life would merely consist of a restless search for a poor substitute of what I had once, briefly, enjoyed.

In truth, I still have that fear. A year is not sufficient time to build a new life. I am able to see the outlines of it, to know that I want eventually to move home, pursue some form of training in counselling and above all else find another remarkable woman to love. And I know that when I finally establish that new life I will savour every moment of it. But I do not yet know the detail of it, or how, when or even if, I will achieve it.

I do, however, know enough to be clear about one thing. This is a journey which *can* be navigated. We may not realise it until we turn round and look back to see how far we have come, but even within the first year – slowly, almost imperceptibly – daily living becomes easier; the shock, rawness and physical pain subsides and we begin the long process of readjustment. The strength of human resilience is a remarkable and humbling thing.

So, therefore, I now share my journey through the first year surviving suicide and widowhood in order to offer others on a similar path both the reassurance that they are not alone in their distress and the hope that it can and will be survived. It *is* possible to live again.

There is, of course, one other, very personal, reason, for this book. It has become obvious to me during the course of this cruellest of years that grief is, essentially, about love. It cannot exist without its oxygen. This is, therefore, my token of love for my beautiful wife, my means of honouring her. Regardless of the pain and trauma I have experienced these past months, and the sadness that I will now always hold within me, for the privilege of having been Louise's husband – I remain the luckiest man in the world.

Carry on Breathing

23rd February | 31 days

My apologies to anybody who may be reading this in the hope that it will contain tributes to Sid James, Kenneth Williams or Hattie Jacques. I am afraid that you will be disappointed. Much as I loved the 'Carry On' series as a child, the reference to Carry on Breathing relates not to a previously undiscovered film comedy classic but the best advice I have so far come across for dealing with the immediate aftermath of the suicide of your partner.

People often advise those who have experienced bereavement to 'take each day as it comes'. It's a well-worn and well-intentioned mantra, which is no doubt useful further down the path on the long road to be travelled. But it's actually wholly inadequate for the lightning bolt shock of the early days and weeks.

As I sat in the ambulance outside my house on the night I came home to discover that Louise had taken her life, being fussed over by kindly paramedics and questioned apologetically and gently by police officers, my mind was a swirling, reeling mix of thoughts and worries, some with enormous implications, some ludicrously trivial, some coherent, some not, some justified, some not.

All I could really take in was that my life had been transformed, utterly and irrevocably, in an instant. I had gone to work in the morning with a wonderful, physically-fit 40-year-old wife, the financial security that comes from two very respectable salaries, a modest but pleasant home which felt safe and secure, and a future life which seemed set to take a predictable path involving more of the same that we had enjoyed together over the previous four-and-a-half years.

Now, in the time it took me to read the note Louise left for me on the front door, trying to protect me, warning me to call the emergency services before entering the house and not to come in alone, everything was gone. I couldn't even begin at that stage to take in the enormity of Louise's death, the emotional torment and physical pain she had suffered and the fact that I would never see her again. Exactly one month on, I still haven't properly processed any of that. But even in my stupor I was able to realise that nothing would ever be the same again, that all the certainties had been overturned and replaced with a complete void. The short term was as unknowable as the long term.

In these circumstances, a day was an impossibly distant horizon. I had no idea how I would get from one minute to the next, let alone think in hours. The fortnight leading up to the funeral crept by in similar fashion, one heart-wrenching, inconceivable trauma after another; the night without sleep on my sister's sofa, the return home the following day, the first night in bed without Louise alongside me, the phone calls to inform family and friends, the visit to the undertakers to arrange the funeral, dealing with the coroners, the day of the post mortem and the knowledge throughout it of what was happening to Louise's wonderful body which I had held and loved so many times. Then came my final visit to say goodbye the day prior to the funeral, followed by the committal at the Crematorium and subsequent Memorial Service.

Each of these events, and the overwhelming sensations of grief, loss, guilt and bewilderment, needed to be endured, or at least survived. For once in my life the internet couldn't present a solution. No matter how many Google searches I undertook, none would be able to bring Louise back, allow us to do the 23rd of January differently.

But I did stumble across a coping mechanism. I forget where, so unfortunately I can't attribute it. The advice, however, was simply to keep breathing. This instantly made sense. When everything was too much, too complicated, just too enormous to deal with, all I needed to do was concentrate on breathing. It's simple; even I was capable of that. Breathe once, then again and again and gradually the minutes, hours and days pass on their own. There was no need to go out and meet them. They would happen of their own accord and come to me. No pressure, no expectation, just the steady passage of time as I travelled through the eye of the storm.

I can't pretend that this was transformative, that it made the process bearable. Of course it didn't. But it did provide me, for the first time since the already far distant and untouchable golden days before the 23rd of January, with at least an illusion of control over events. A tool to help me get by. A tiny, hopelessly inadequate tool, but a tool nevertheless and for that I was extremely grateful.

Still Dead

25th February | 33 days

Every day I wake up and every day it's the same. Louise is still dead.

I can't get my head around the concept. I genuinely find it baffling. There are large chunks of the day when I get by. When I'm feeling a general sadness but I'm not on the verge of tears. I can function. But I know that is because the reality of what has happened, the sheer hugeness of it all, the tragedy of it all, and the permanence of the loss, hasn't remotely sunk in.

Every time, something pierces that veneer of protection; I sit bewildered, and try to come to terms with the reality all over again, struggling to take in the enormity and to understand what it means. It's almost as if the news that Louise has died is broken to me afresh several times a day.

In a sense, my brain is working on two levels. It understands the fact that Louise has died. It has to accept the evidence. My memories of that night, of finding Louise hanging from the bannisters, seeing her in the chapel of rest, the committal at the crematorium, the memorial service, her absence from the house, the lack of text messages from her. So I know all this. And yet I can't absorb it. Don't understand it.

I get frustrated by my inability to process what has happened. I feel as though I'm being stupid for not grasping it. Yet, it's actually better this way. It helps me absorb the shock, to continue to cope. It holds me up off the floor. Sometimes. Until something breaks through the protective layer. Like just now.

I've picked up the post and found that the bank have sent me a new cheque book. It only has my name on the account. A further piece of evidence of Louise's existence, and of our union, is removed. Louise takes another step backwards into the past. As does my marriage. The relentless and inevitable efficiency of bureaucracy moves things on at its own pace, not mine.

I can control the speed with which the process of saying goodbye to Louise takes place in my house – whether and when to move this item out of sight or to throw that item away. But I can't do anything to slow down the outside world and its apparent desire to rearrange things in the new correct order as quickly as possible, before I am ready for it.

I wept all over again. I've now been crying for more than 30 days.

Losing the Past

2nd March | 38 days

It seems that every day I discover new aspects of loss. I was thinking this morning of all the wonderful holidays Louise and I enjoyed together. We were fortunate that we had sufficient time and disposable income to take two holidays and, usually, a couple of weekend breaks a year. We were probably able to experience more in our four-and-a-half years together than many couples do in twice that time. I am blessed with a precious store chest of memories and photographs, for which I am very grateful.

Until now I have concentrated on the future that I have lost. I have been painfully aware that there will be no more of these holidays, no more of the things that we planned to do. We will never take that trip to Cuba, return to Kardamyli in the Peloponnese, enjoy road trips around Europe or share holidays together with friends in French gites. I will never be able to surprise Louise with the big present of a VW camper van that I so much wanted to be able to give her one day.

And of course it's not just holidays. It's our whole shared future together that has been lost, everything that we planned to do with the house, the plays we were going to see, the books we were going to read, the films we were going to watch, the time with family and friends, the Christmases we were going to enjoy, the season ticket we were going to get Louise so that she could more regularly join me at Brentford matches. Most of all, the love that we were going to share, the support we would give each other, the nights we would spend cuddled up in bed together, the unexpected joys we would experience together, the sadness and disappointments we would work through with each other.

All this has gone and I've been acutely conscious of that loss from the first few moments. But what I hadn't really thought about much – until now – is the way the past has been so badly impaired that it almost feels that it too has been taken from me. Our time together was so short that none of the memories have sanctuary from the darkness of the ending. Had our relationship stretched for 10 or 20 years – not long in the great scheme of things but something which seems to me now to be an unimaginable length of time together – then there would have been a period at the beginning when those memories were not tinged with knowledge of the pain and horror to come. They could live on pure and unsullied.

As it is, however, four-and-a-half years offers no hiding place. Even the photos of our wedding three-and-a-half years ago are now inevitably tainted with the thought of what was to happen so soon after. The brevity of our time together is sharply illustrated by the fact that many of the clothes we can be seen wearing in our earliest photos can also be seen in some of the last. Our relationship had the lifespan of an M&S shirt.

But there is something else which also robs me of the past I treasured so much and thought was securely stored forever; something which could never be taken from me. Without Louise, the person present in all those moments, I have nobody to share my memories with. There is nobody I can talk to about those times, who knows what it was like to be in the moment, who can recall what we did, what we said and how we were feeling, to reflect it back to me. Nobody to whom I can relive and enhance the memories by saying 'do you remember when…?'

Somehow, having nobody to bear witness to memory almost serves to invalidate it. The facts of what happened remain but the happiness which surrounded the most precious moments of my life has disappeared. Perhaps, in time, I will feel differently and be able to reclaim those memories for what they should be, but at present it feels as though I haven't just lost my future but also my past.

Reading Louise's Mind

3rd March | 39 days

Louise's mind was never still. Always thinking, always challenging, always seeking the truth but always realistic enough to recognise that when she found it, there was likely only to be ambiguity and uncertainty. It gave her great wisdom and insight and an acute awareness of, and identification with, the needs of others. It was what made her so passionate about championing the socially excluded and was partly why she was such an effective and popular doctor. Louise would spend hours at the end of the working day reviewing case notes and re-thinking earlier consultations. This would often provide her with fresh insight and lead to improved outcomes for her patients, who loved her for it.

When Louise was struggling with her periodic episodes of depression, however, this analysis and reflection was focused internally. She worked ceaselessly to reach an understanding of her condition, its causes, its symptoms and the factors which led her to recovery on each occasion. As a consequence, the house is filled with notebooks in which Louise attempted to set down her thinking, metaphorically stripping herself bare and examining every aspect of her inner self. Her laptop is similarly well-populated with documents performing the same function.

I can't help but come across these notes from time to time. Before Louise died, I would never have even contemplated looking at them. They were intended for Louise's private use. She would and did share her thoughts with me on a very regular basis but these were the refined conclusions she had reached from the rough working in her notebooks. I respected the space Louise needed to get to that point.

But now I have a dilemma, and like many dilemmas I am suddenly confronted with, I have no answer to it. Do I now have the right, or perhaps even the duty, to read these notes? I want to understand, need to understand, why Louise decided she had no option but to kill herself (or rather, why the illness led her to believe that she had no other option — there was no free will pursued here). Insight on this may help me come to terms with events. It should help me better understand the most cataclysmic event ever to hit myself or those I love. Surely I have a right to know what it is that has taken my wife from me and reduced me to a state of despair?

And yet surely Louise also retains a right to her privacy even now? There is no 'read upon my death' instruction scrawled across the front covers of the notebooks. Just because Louise is no longer here, do I really have the right to examine every aspect of her most private thoughts? And if I did, would it really be helpful to me? I am having difficulty enough dealing with my own grief, loss and guilt. The only way that I can do this is to block out from my mind the very worst aspect of all, which is the pain and torment Louise suffered. I saw the effects of that darkness. I know what it did to her on a day-to-day basis when she was at her lowest ebb. And of course I possess and re-read, almost daily, her lengthy farewell letter to me which summarised her turmoil.

But to expose myself to the daily fluctuations of her raw, unprocessed innermost fears and feelings, and at a time when there is no longer an opportunity to respond to them, to reassure and support the woman that I love so much, would surely be a particularly cruel form of self-punishment. If I open the door even slightly to Louise's torment there is no telling what it may do.

So, for the time being, I am securely preserving the notebooks and backing up the Word files. This is partly because the more of Louise's voice I keep, the more alive she remains, but also partly because I haven't resolved the question of what I can or should do with them. I know that I can't bring myself to look at them yet but I may need to do so at some point in the future when I am better able to deal with what I will find. Or it may be that I will never have the strength, but our nephews and nieces subsequently want to learn more about why they have been deprived of their wonderful Aunt.

Perhaps we will understand more in time, but now is not the moment.

Going to the Match

4th March | 40 days

It's now nearly six weeks since Louise died and I still spend virtually every waking moment (and many sleeping moments) thinking about and analysing the events of 23rd January and the implications. It's both emotionally and physically exhausting to focus so intensely on something for so long almost without any distraction. I can't open a book or watch TV because I just wouldn't be able to concentrate. In any event, Louise and I almost never watched TV so having the set on would only serve to emphasise the abnormality and Louise's absence. I avoid complete silence around the house with music but can't play my favourite tracks since most would have an association of some description with Louise.

But there is one thing which is beginning to offer me some escape. My beloved Brentford Football Club.

Louise always wished that she too could enjoy an overriding passion or interest which she could immerse herself in and which would enable her to find a complete release from the pressures of work. Perhaps if she had, she might have been better equipped to deal with her episodes of depression. A hobby or interest in which she could fully engage would have provided her with a means of switching off, escaping from the anxiety and perhaps diverting her overactive mind. But true to gender stereotypes, Louise had a variety of diverse interests which she enjoyed but held lightly whereas I have a small number of all-consuming passions.

Brentford is so embedded in my life, and has been since the age of five, that resuming the ritual of going to watch them play was always going to be my primary route back to some form of routine and normality. The first home match came a week after Louise's death. I didn't want to go. I didn't feel remotely ready and the very idea of doing something which wasn't directly mourning Louise seemed entirely inappropriate.

But I had posted a thread about Louise on a supporters' message board forum and received such a tremendously warm and supportive response that I almost felt obliged to attend. Louise's brother strongly encouraged me and I knew that Louise herself would have wanted me to go. Once I learned that, coincidentally, the match would be preceded by the annual minute's applause for all supporters who had passed away over the previous 12 months I knew that I had to be there.

So I went and through the tears clapped my heart out for Louise and then took in nothing that happened afterwards. For the first few matches, I felt completely separated from the occasion. Things that had been routine, that I took for granted, suddenly seemed alien. I remember walking through the turnstiles at Griffin Park and making my way to my regular seat feeling bemused by the crowds and the noise and colour. I was in the crowd but not part of it. I sat through the matches and mechanically followed the path of the ball but couldn't remotely engage with what I was seeing. I didn't care about the result. Ironically, almost the hardest part was when Brentford scored. As the crowd celebrated wildly, I stood and gently applauded for the sake of form. It's an odd thing to experience such a gulf between my emotions and those of 10,000 other people around me, particularly when normally they are in perfect harmony

In theory, going to the match should have been my private space, something which I could do as I had always done. Something which was not reliant on Louise and, therefore, one of the very few things which could relatively quickly return to normality.

But Brentford had come to play a very significant and symbolic role in our life as a couple. Louise had no interest in football when we met but such was her wholehearted, enthusiastic and generous nature she didn't just want to tolerate my hobbies but to actively join me in them. She would come with me to three or four matches a season. She didn't always follow the detail or the tactics of a match and sometimes she found the sheer intensity of emotion engendered by the crowd so difficult to deal with that she couldn't watch the game at all.

Yet Louise intuitively recognised how important it all was to me. She was willing not just to allow me to go to matches, but actively encouraged me to spend some Saturdays travelling to long-distance away fixtures because she knew it was an important part of my response to the stresses of life. Even the day before she died, she was trying to encourage me to travel on the following weekend to a match at Norwich on the grounds that I needed an escape from the stress of trying to support her through her crisis.

Louise responded to the sense of community the club invoked among its supporters, a concept which was so close to her heart. She readily saw the parallels with the church communities which had played such a large part in most of her life. She was rather touched (and slightly amused) by the way in which a largely male and working class constituency used the medium of football to haltingly attempt to communicate with each other emotionally, whether at the match or in online forums.

Even when Louise wasn't at a match she would send regular texts asking me to 'give the Bees a cheer from me' and the final whistle would be sure to see a text with an appropriate comment on the result. By the time I got home Louise would invariably have read a report of the game so that she could ask me informed questions about it.

All this was essentially an expression of Louise's love for me and desire for us to join together in activities as a couple. Therefore, far from being in my own self-contained sphere, I feel as close to Louise's love at a Brentford match as I do anywhere else.

I feel guilty for admitting this but at the most recent game, on Tuesday evening, I found myself participating in the occasion. Not as passionately as I normally would, of course, but enough to feel connected to what was happening around me. Thoughts of Louise were never far away but for 90 minutes my mind had something else to occupy it for the first time in six weeks. It was a wonderful relief to experience some sense of normality but, at the same time, a weight on my conscience. How could I allow myself any pleasure when the woman I loved with all my heart was no longer alive? Surely I hadn't forgotten?

At the final whistle I could keep it up no longer. I ached to receive Louise's usual post-match text and walked back to the car as quickly as I could, trying to lose the crowds around me so as to prevent anybody seeing the tears. By the time I reached the privacy of the car I was fit to burst, and did.

It feels wrong to know that that, if nothing else, I can now partly escape and lose myself in something else for 90 minutes once a week. But I know that Louise would both understand and wholeheartedly approve.

The Empty Bed

When I was first grasping for language and imagery which would somehow convey the scale of my loss and grief, I tried to describe things by saying that Louise's death profoundly affected every aspect of my life from the moment I got up to the moment I went to bed. But of course that is only half the story because it omits the seven or eight hours in-between which are the most intimate of any marriage.

In many ways it is precisely the period overnight when the loss of your partner is most obvious and stark. For much of the day it is relatively easy to explain away Louise's absence – she is in another room, at work or out at the shops. We wouldn't normally expect to be together the whole time. But in the middle of the night, no such false reassurance can be found. The empty half of the bed to my left screams loss. Where I naturally expect to find the solid, warm and tender presence of Louise's body next to me, now there is just a void. As I stare across at the empty side it almost feels as though I am looking at myself with a limb cut off. Something natural and human which is integral to me isn't any longer where it should be.

Six weeks ago I went to bed with my wonderful wife every evening. The sharing of a bed signified love and togetherness and provided both warmth and comfort. Cold nights were made for snuggling up with each other. Nightmares were soothed instantly upon waking through the reassurance of knowing that Louise was there with me. No harm could come to me. No ghosts or spirits or demons could frighten me when I had my wife by my side.

Now, however, my companions are a hot water bottle to keep me warm and a low nightlight to help feel secure. Even my dog generally disobligingly refuses to sleep on the bed to provide at least some company. When I wake from a nightmare, not only am I alone, I also remember that it's true.

I struggled for a while to establish how to deal with the space next to me. I tried sleeping in the middle of the bed but that simply isn't practical for reaching the bedside table. It also meant moving Louise's pyjamas which, for the first few weeks, lay where she had left them, on her pillows. I considered sleeping on Louise's own side of the bed since it would therefore no longer be empty, but this felt too much like crowding her out.

I even tried placing a pillow in the bed where Louise lay in order to reduce the sensation of emptiness but, if anything, this was too effective. Louise often lay on a pillow to prevent twinges in her back and waking up on a morning to find a pillow once more next to me induced a split-second illusion of normality which was reassuring for its duration but cruel the moment reality imposed itself.

So now I have accepted that the bed will remain lopsided, with me occupying only my normal half of it. This has its advantages. Most notably, by preserving Louise's half of the bed as distinct and separate it has come to represent the physical focal point for my grieving, a surrogate for a grave.

It's my main point of communication with Louise. While I talk to her all the time, when I want to say anything particularly significant I head upstairs and sit on the bed, addressing her side of it. When I wanted to show Louise the DVD of her memorial service, to explain to her exactly how loved and well-regarded she was by so many people, and to show her my eulogy, I placed the laptop in front of her pillow and pressed play. When a new photobook of one of our last holidays arrived recently, I put it in the same position and turned the pages to show Louise the entire book.

None of this might be rational but, as any number of people have advised me, the key to surviving bereavement is to do whatever it takes to find comfort, no matter how silly it may seem to others.

In time, I might come up with a better solution. But it certainly won't be a single bed. This was, and is, our marital bed and since in my heart I am still very much married to Louise, I draw some comfort from continuing to use it. Whilst it's true that the emptiness of the bed starkly illustrates our enforced separation, it also remains a potent symbol and reminder of our time together and enduring love. It is therefore a place where I can strongly feel (or imagine) Louise's presence. Somehow she manages in the bed to seem both so far away and so close simultaneously.

Living With the House

8th March | 44 days

Louise and I moved into our current house less than two years ago. It was the first place that we had bought together as a couple and we intended to stay here for the rest of our lives. I will now always treasure the photo of Louise about to cross the threshold for the first time on the day we moved in. It was just a snapshot taken on my phone but it perfectly captures a moment of happiness, excitement and high hopes for the future life we were going to create together.

But on the night that Louise died the house represented something else altogether. As my sister drove me out of the road I stared back at my home. It had been a place of such light, love, warmth, comfort and security. Now I saw a variety of police cars and ambulances, lights flashing, pulled up outside. Forensics officers were inspecting my lounge and kitchen and my wonderful wife, the love of my life, was still where I had found her, awaiting the arrival of a different kind of photographer to the one she normally posed in front of so obligingly and lovingly. Not me, but one employed by the police.

If ever a scene conveyed the wreckage of two peoples' lives this was it. I thought that on top of everything else I was homeless. I would never be able to return to the house again.

And yet by the following morning I was desperate to get back. It was the home we shared together, the place where I could be closest to Louise. I needed to be there.

Within 14 hours of leaving, I was walking through the front door again, this time in the supportive presence of the rest of my family. There were plenty of signs of what had happened the previous evening and plenty of things to find that Louise had carefully left for me, including her farewell letter (thoughtfully prepared on her laptop as hard copy notes tend to be taken by the police as part of their investigations), her wedding and engagement rings, and a pack of papers about her financial affairs.

The process of discovery continued over the next few days; notebooks Louise had been writing her thoughts in, notes she had scribbled on pieces of paper, and emails she had sent at various times during that final day, some indicating that she was planning to live, others that she was planning to die. It was a truly heart-rending experience, piecing together her movements and her emotions.

But I also had to deal with rediscovering what had, up until 24 hours before, been the mundane and everyday but which was now the unutterably poignant; Louise's pyjamas folded neatly on the pillow next to mine, her washing on the clothes dryer, the CD left in the stereo ready to play, the half-completed shopping list, the calendar filled with appointments and events Louise would now never attend, the remnants of our last dinner together still on the plates in the kitchen, our last Christmas cards to each other…

And so it went on. Living amongst all these reminders was intensely painful and emotional but it was also completely necessary. I had offers to stay with friends elsewhere but never considered taking them up. I immediately recognised that I needed to be as close to Louise as possible and this was where I could do that. I couldn't live in the house but I couldn't live elsewhere. All those painful reminders were also comforting symbols of normality. A lost normality but one that I could fool myself into believing still existed if I was around them. This was, and remains, enormously comforting.

Now that the weeks have passed and the friends and family who initially stayed with me have returned to their own homes, leaving me here alone, I am more certain than ever that I made the right choice to return, and to do so quickly. It's true that from mid-evening onwards I tend to feel slightly edgy, particularly around the hallway, but essentially I am surprised about how relatively relaxed I am about the house, especially in daylight. The only real modification I have made to my habits is to keep more lights on than normal, and to turn them on in advance when I am going out so that I don't have to return to a completely dark house.

Friends have commented that the house feels much lighter than they expected. Maybe having a lively dog around the place helps to ensure it still feels like a home. Or maybe the fact that as soon as I walked through the front door for the first time afterwards, I instinctively hugged the bannisters where I had last seen Louise helps to bring peace around them. It wasn't planned, but even now, when I am at my most distressed I find myself drawn to the same place, to hug Louise in her crisis.

At present, I think I would find it very difficult to leave. That may change if I start getting flashbacks but for the moment this is a space where I can still feel connected with Louise. I can, at least in part, control the pace at which she moves from the present to the future and ensure that it only moves as fast as I am able to deal with it. Currently the vast majority of her possessions remain exactly as they were left. I am trying, with only partial success, to tidy or throw away one small item every day so that the change is almost imperceptible and emotionally manageable.

Or at least relatively so. I have just been to the shops and needed to find space in the freezer. I had to tackle the task I have been putting off, throwing away Louise's food, items which I don't eat and which were now well out of date anyway. Looking at the pile of discarded food in the bin, it somehow felt as though I was starving her by depriving her of it. Another precious sign of Louise's everyday life had disappeared. Another part of her had died. It seems to happen bit by excruciating bit. I had my worst breakdown in a week or so.

But despite the cumulative effect of these individual losses, when I glance around the house it still looks fairly normal, as if Louise is just in another room or has popped out to the shops. Whilst I don't consciously play along with the deceit, I know that I need it in order to get through. My heart is not ready for Louise to die and in this house, if nowhere else, it feels as though she hasn't. I know that I am fighting a losing battle but I am determined to continue the struggle until time permits me the grace of acceptance.

Anger (and Love)

9th March | 45 days

Everything that I have read about bereavement suggests that anger is a natural emotional response to the death of a loved one. Perhaps this might be expected to be particularly true in the case of suicide. How could my partner have done this to themself? How could they have been so selfish and done this to me? How could they have left me with all this to deal with, not just now but for the rest of my life?

And yet my only source of anger stems from the frustration that I have nobody to be angry with. Except, that is, for myself – for my own failings in the last few days of Louise's life. For the decisions that I made which seemed – at the time – to be entirely reasonable but, with the benefit of hindsight, proved to be wrong. For the things which I could have done but didn't. And for the failure to recognise the signs. Ultimately, for my inability to be able to perform the most basic duty of any husband; to keep his wife safe. But this is more guilt than anger, a topic which, if I ever have the strength, I will return to because it haunts me day and night.

I feel no anger towards Louise. I couldn't. Anger wasn't a part of our relationship. Neither Louise nor I found the emotion easy to deal with. For some couples it can be a healthy release mechanism, a way of working things out. Not us. It wasn't in our natures. We had other effective means for resolving our differences. I can truthfully say that we never once had an argument. We certainly had some difficult conversations but they were always controlled, measured and respectful. The only time that I ever raised my voice to Louise was a week before she died, when she suggested that it might be better for me if she killed herself.

But more significantly, I can have no anger towards Louise because I understand why she took her life. The greatest strength of our relationship was the way in which we talked and communicated emotionally. I could never presume to be able to fully understand what it is like to be inside the head of somebody suffering from deep anxiety and depression, let alone the kind of darkness which eventually leads them to believe that the best course of action is to kill themself. But I think that I got as close as possible. Louise herself used to take great comfort in the fact that I understood her.

As a consequence, I could never blame her for what she did, no matter what the implications are for me. I know that Louise worked incredibly hard, fought so bravely over the years against the episodic depression and anxiety she suffered. And I know that in the final weeks, and even into the final days, hours and moments, she was continuing to fight to keep alive the will to live.

Ultimately, she lost that fight. But it wasn't through her choice. She suffered from an illness as insidious and dangerous as a cancer and eventually it proved too strong for her. But there was no weakness of character and even the final act was, in its own way, as brave a thing to do as anything I can possibly imagine. Certainly braver than anything I would ever have been able to do. Sometimes it's not the weak who die by suicide but the strong.

Of course it was wrong. Louise had so much to live for but her illness had caused her thinking to become momentarily muddled. At the time she killed herself she did it because she genuinely didn't want to continue living the way she was feeling in that moment, and because she genuinely thought that it was the best thing to do for me; to release me from the strain of supporting her.

It was, in many ways, an act of supreme self-sacrifice. I could no more be angry with Louise for eventually losing this fight against such a powerful force than I could had she lost her life to cancer. On the contrary. I was always incredibly proud of Louise and, if anything, that pride is enhanced even further because of my sheer admiration for her courage, dignity, strength and generosity throughout her illness.

But this means that I have nobody to be angry with. And that leaves me frustrated because I have anger within me and no outlet for it. I want to scream at the injustice of Louise losing her life, of the world losing such a wonderful force for goodness, of me losing the person I had just so recently found and thought had completed my life at long last.

I suppose that I could turn that anger towards God. But that presupposes a relationship with Him of the type where I hold Him accountable for all human destiny. My Christian faith is not of that type. I have hope in the existence of an inclusive greater being of infinite wisdom, love, mercy, understanding and compassion. I pray daily, even in normal circumstances, and especially so at this time. But I have no certainty. I cannot find it in myself to blame God for a human ailment, even one which modern medical science still understands so imperfectly.

So I find it difficult dealing with anger. But it's interesting, and of some comfort, to reflect on what I have just written and find that although I set out to write about anger, the emotion which continues to overwhelm me is actually love.

Let's Talk About Sex

11th March | 47 days

That instinctively doesn't sound right does it? Over the course of the past few weeks I've read extensively about bereavement and coping with the loss of a partner. And one subject that seems to be rarely addressed is the sense of loss the surviving partner experiences for the sexual relationship we enjoyed with our loved one.

I can see why this is. In our memory of them, our natural need to remember and celebrate the positive aspects of our partner, sees them become idealised, almost sanctified. The ritual of mourning serves to strengthen this further; the tributes from family, friends and colleagues, the memorial service, the way in which, for those with faith, or at least hope of faith, God and the Church become almost the intermediary between us and our partners as we begin to communicate with them, or about them, through prayer and worship and hope for heavenly happiness.

There is a wonderful purity about this remembrance. Yet our real life relationships with our partners were built on messier, more human and down-to-earth emotions and needs. And however much it might jar now, part of that was about the physical relationship.

The screensaver on my laptop is a photo of Louise and me taken at my sister's house at Christmas a couple of years ago. It's one of my favourite photos of Louise because it captures her at her most beautiful and radiant. I love the way that she had her hair that day, she was wearing a dress that always made me fancy her like mad and her smile and eyes perfectly captured her kindness and gentleness. I look at it now and I feel a deep craving for her.

This almost feels wrong, inappropriate. As if it risks spoiling the purity of my love because of baser human need. Yet it's a reality. As I suppose is the case in all good marriages, after the passing of the initial high intensity passion, sex was, for us, primarily an expression of our love for each other. It was about warmth, tenderness and togetherness. I know that Louise would express it in that way. There can nothing to be ashamed about in this.

And there is nothing to be ashamed about in having continuing longing and desires for our partners. We are human and our needs and emotions don't die with our loved one. They survive with us.

This is only natural, perhaps particularly so in the case of suicide. We didn't decide to divorce or separate. There was no loss of love. We didn't choose to be parted from each other ('choice' in suicide implies a free will that surely cannot exist alongside the torment and desperation of the darkest of depression). Nor was there a long period of physical illness prior to our partner's death which perhaps accustomed us to a lack of physicality in our lives. Our loss was involuntary and sudden. Our feelings for our partner remain intact. Perhaps they are even heightened by the intensity of our emotional state as we experience bereavement.

In the immediate aftermath we are so shocked, so numbed, that perhaps there is no room for any thoughts about the physical relationship. They are crowded out by too many other things. At least, that was the way it was for me. But as the weeks go by, it's inevitable that we become aware that amongst all the other loss, the warmth and love and togetherness of our physical relationship is now also denied us. What was once ours is now completely unattainable.

I have no answer to this. I am confused about how I should feel and deal with it. It feels slightly shocking and wrong to learn that I can have an intense physical attraction and desire for somebody who is dead. Yet, at the same time, it's entirely right and appropriate because it's another expression of my continuing love for Louise, another compliment to my wonderful wife.

It reminds me yet again, as if I needed further reminding, that Louise's loss truly and deeply affects every single facet of my existence and every single need and emotion. And it also presents problems and dilemmas that I had never previously imagined but which are now real, urgent and bewildering.

Helpless

12th March | 48 days

I have just looked out of the kitchen window and noticed flowers Louise planted in the garden beginning to come through. She will never see them. I have broken down again.

In a sense, I can deal with my loss. I know that however bad it is now, things will eventually get a little easier and I will go on to have some form of other life. Not as emotionally rich or as textured as the one that I thought awaited me, but something.

But I can do nothing now about the pain and suffering Louise experienced, or all the events and happiness that she will miss out on as the years progress. That is infinitely harder than my own selfish grief. I love Louise with all my heart and I cannot cope with the thought of her torment. If I could do anything to alleviate it for her, if I could take her place, I would. But I'm powerless to help her any more.

Thinking the Unthinkable

15th March | 51 days

A few days ago I thought that I was making some progress. Some of the rawness and immediacy of the shock and grief had worn off. There were intervals when I was able to concentrate on other things, slowly re-engaging with some of my interests. I was beginning to lift my head a little, to think about the short-term future. I made arrangements to return to work, started to consider what I might do to occupy my spare time and even began to contemplate a holiday later in the year.

I still broke down several times a day. The tears didn't stop and there was obviously no happiness. But neither, for much of the day, was there an overwhelming sense of sadness or despair. I found myself thinking 'I can survive this'.

I even had the luxury of worrying that I was coping too well, to feel guilty for my lack of obvious distress. I began to wonder what Louise might think of this apparent indifference just six weeks after her death. It caused me to challenge myself, question how I could have forgotten so quickly and worry that it meant I didn't really care. When I did cry, I felt almost a sense of relief. Not only that the sadness and despair I felt inside me had been temporarily purged, but also because it validated my grief; it proved to me, the world and, most importantly, to Louise that I genuinely cared. That this really did hurt.

But as the self-centred preoccupation with my own loss, grief and suffering has subsided a little, it has created space for me to begin to think about Louise's torment and loss, which is infinitely harder to deal with. Up until now, I have managed to keep the door to that part of my brain firmly locked. I have known that the demons which lie within are much more powerful and debilitating than those I have had to contend with on my own account. Nevertheless, it is becoming harder and harder to resist the compulsion to open the door and confront the darkest conceivable thoughts.

I am therefore now struggling to contend with the reality of the mental and physical torment Louise suffered during those final days and moments. I quite quickly managed to establish her thought processes and movements over the last few hours of her life from the trail of evidence left behind in terms of her notes, the farewell letter, emails, text messages and bank transactions. I know what she did and why. I know from where everything was left when I returned home what Louise did in the house while she made her final preparations. I have a mental image in my mind, almost a video recording, of the sequence of her movements and actions.

Increasingly, I am overlaying on that factual record a sense of Louise's emotions at the time. I am beginning to visualise her last moments and the act itself. To viscerally feel her emotion and struggle. I cannot wholly suppress my imagination and endlessly replay various alternative scenarios around the events of that evening, some of which end with Louise's survival, others not. All are deeply distressing and leave me feeling emotionally exhausted.

Of course, in addition to Louise's pain in the moment, there is also her long-term loss. The sense of all the love, happiness and achievement that she will miss out on over the years.

The hesitant signs of the emergence of spring with its new life and hope somehow intensifies the thought. Every sunny day, every new flower causes me to shudder afresh at the thought that Louise won't see it, or anything like it, ever again. I have just come across a text Louise sent me earlier in the winter when she had planted some daffodils and told me she 'was looking forward to spring'. And I have the certain knowledge that had Louise managed to survive the darkness of those few days, she would now be back at work, happy and fulfilled, making plans for the future and carrying on her life with her usual zest and energy. I can hear her say to me now, as she did so many times after coming through a depressive episode, 'I am so lucky and so happy'.

I desperately want to make everything better, to ease Louise's torment, to fulfil the role that I thought had been assigned to me in life, to help and support the woman I loved so dearly and who gave me so much in return.

I feel Louise's pain even more acutely than my own. Broken though my life is at the moment, I at least have a second chance, an opportunity to rebuild and repair. I will still be able to see and experience the changing seasons, enjoy holidays and, if I am very lucky, maybe one day experience again the joy, beauty and warmth of another loving relationship.

It will be different and my life will be forever poorer. The scar tissue which superficially covers the wound will always be tender and perpetually liable to re-open. But nevertheless, I retain the potential for some kind of future. Louise doesn't. The pain this causes me is beyond description.

Counting my Blessings

19th March | 55 days

It's curious how misery is so often perceived as being relative rather than absolute. We hear on countless occasions the phrase 'there is always somebody worse off than you'. And we take comfort in this, as if it's a zero sum game – another person's suffering can somehow alleviate our own. After weeks of solemnly being told that Louise's death is a tragedy, I still find it difficult to mentally categorise either of us as tragic figures. Tragedy is something that happens to other people. Those who died or were injured in the Hillsborough disaster, the World Trade Centre attacks, the Lockerbie bombing. They were caught up in tragedy.

Louise? Well, she was Louise, my wife. The person with whom I shared my life. Somebody so close to me clearly can't be caught up in tragedy, and nor can I. That would be absurd. Utterly inconceivable. Obviously, something has happened to take Louise away from me for several weeks now, and I'm not yet sure what it is. I'm missing her, an awful lot, but she is bound to be back any minute now.

Despite this ironclad protective layer of disbelief, however, reality still penetrates fairly frequently. Generally at least two or three times a day. And then I wonder what I have done to deserve being in this position. But if I start feeling too sorry for myself I try to pause and take a moment to count my blessings. It requires only a quick perusal of web forums for those who have lost their partners, whether by suicide or not (I now spend more time on these than my football club's message board) to establish that I do, in fact, still have many reasons to consider myself fortunate.

Unlike some, for example, I am lucky enough to have a reasonably sound financial outlook. Not what it would have been, of course, but there should still be no reason why I have to sell my home or experience a dramatic drop in living standards. I don't have the strain of trying to bring up one or more children as a single parent at the same time as dealing with my bereavement. My employers have been appropriately supportive and accommodating. And Louise's family and friends, and of course my own, have rallied around to collectively embrace me.

I have, through talking to those family and friends, and the writing of this book, opportunities and resources which enable me to process and work through my understanding of what happened and why. There are exciting plans for the establishment of a new charity which will provide Louise with a fitting legacy.

I have not been left with a whole series of unanswered questions about why Louise did what she did. I know and understand. I am secure in the fact that Louise loved me and wants the best for me. And I know that I am still the luckiest man in the world for having had the absolute honour and privilege of being her husband.

Of course I would be lying if I tried to pretend that this lifts me up off the floor, either literally or figuratively, when I am having a breakdown. It doesn't. But in-between times, it provides me with a valuable sense of perspective and puts a break on the emergence of any form of victimhood. I may be cursed but I know that I am also blessed.

Two Months

23rd March | 59 days

Louise's death provides me with a new reference point from which I measure the passage of time and my own personal development. In a sense a new self was born on 23rd January; wiser, sadder, hopefully more gentle, loving and understanding and with different ambitions and goals to the one that had existed before. There is no other single event in my life which has so defined and reshaped me – and will no doubt continue to do so in ways which I cannot currently imagine.

I have become used to thinking of this new life in terms of weeks – three weeks since Louise died, four, five, six… But now I am surprised to realise that it's two months. I'm not quite sure how I've managed to get to this point, the time seems both to have crawled and sped along. And whilst in some respects I welcome the distance that is now emerging between that hideous day and the present, the protective barrier that time erects, I am also deeply saddened by it because it represents an ever-growing distance between Louise and myself.

It's an odd stage to be at. The all-consuming patterns of grief, shock and mourning in the early days are clear, as are the expectations that some sort of recovery, of new normality, will have asserted itself several months down the line. But, at this point, I'm stuck somewhere in the middle. Everything is still fresh and raw but different patterns and ways of thinking are beginning to emerge.

The collective hug, the love bombing, which I experienced in the time between Louise's death and the funeral from family, friends and almost complete strangers, has ended. No more sympathy cards come through the door. Most of my email is, once more, spam. People remain, by and large, very supportive, some exceptionally so. I shall be grateful to them for the rest of my life. I have been very lucky with mine – and Louise's – friends and family.

But, nevertheless, life inevitably and understandably moves on for others and I am aware of an inequality of grief. Whereas initially all of us who were connected with Louise were in a state of shock, most people have now been able to resume their lives with relatively little daily impact.

That is, of course, completely impossible for me. I remain stuck way behind, still on the starting line of the race for recovery. I'm still in shock, still mourning, albeit perhaps in different and less intense ways from the very early days.

The outward signs of acute shock, the shivering and nausea, have gone, my appetite is largely restored. I am beginning to re-engage with the world around me. I am going to my club's football matches, watching a little cricket on TV, browsing websites for the new camera lenses I have promised to treat myself to, and am beginning to plan a holiday. I have even begun my phased return to work. Now, for periods in the day I feel very little. There is obviously no happiness but neither is there necessarily an overwhelming sense of sadness or despair. I function, albeit with little energy, and can deal with simple day-to-day transactions. I find myself thinking 'I can live this life – it won't be so bad'.

I have surprised myself by how relatively comfortable I am around the house. It still feels like my home and I am increasingly confident even in and around the hallway. Sometimes I am even brave enough to turn the bedroom light off at night. It feels like a place where I can stay. That, at least, is one part of my short- to medium-term future decided.

In essence, I'm getting by. I'm doing okay, or at least as well as could reasonably be expected. The days come to me and I deal with them, which is all I can manage at present.

But the pain and sadness doesn't go away. It just takes different forms, one where the inner hurt is less outwardly apparent. I am tired and lethargic; everything seems such an effort. I frequently carry a knotted, twisted gnawing ache in the pit of my stomach. For the first time in my life, I suffer from night sweats – my pillow is soaked by the time I wake up every morning. It is not a case of whether I will break down and cry each day but when.

I may think that I'm coping well but can suddenly find myself overwhelmed by grief and collapse in tears. Sometimes there are obvious triggers – a photo, a memory, sight of an object around the house, sitting down to eat at the dining room table on my own – but often there is no apparent reason. It can happen anywhere: in the park while walking my dog, while shaving, in the middle of the shops.

Sometimes the tears trickle gently. On other occasions, but much less frequently now, it's a tsunami of hysteria which rises from the pit of my stomach, and twists and racks my whole body to the extent that I physically writhe around, my mouth wide open screaming noiselessly for what seems like an eternity but is probably only a few minutes.

I am still wrapped in a blanket of numbness and shock. I am missing Louise's presence very badly, but in a manner where she might be on holiday and I am expecting her return any moment. I can't accept that she isn't coming back. The concept is too incredible to absorb. I have written the words 'Louise's death' countless times, read and filled out numerous official forms referring to her as 'the late' or 'the deceased' but the words still don't make sense. It's as if they refer to somebody else. It seems like only moments ago that she was standing in front of me, talking, breathing, laughing, loving. Somebody who was so present to me simply cannot be dead.

And I am still overwhelmed by love. I have never known love so intense and pure, so gentle and tender. I always knew that I loved Louise but it's only now, when I know what I am missing, that I fully understand exactly how much she meant to me – and still means to me. Sometimes I think that the pain is not so much because I'm mourning. It's because I'm loving.

I miss her most at night. Sometimes I make the mistake of turning to look to my left, towards Louise's side of the bed. Nothing drives her absence home more than this void in the early hours of the morning. During the day there can be all sorts of reasons why Louise isn't around, but not then. The emptiness screams loss. I try not to touch her part of the bed, partly because when I extend my feet out I expect to meet hers, and partly because the sheets feel so cold and obviously unslept on.

I even miss Louise where she wouldn't normally have been found. When I am at work I keep on involuntarily checking my phone, waiting for her regular texts. It strikes me that bereavement would be much easier to bear if the afterlife had a sufficiently good 4G signal to at least allow regular text communication with this world. And I would be prepared to bet that in those circumstances Louise's celestial mobile phone would still be the simplest handset possible, with her trademark elastic band round it to hold the battery in place.

Most of the house is still untouched from the day Louise died. Most of her possessions remain where they would normally be: visible and ready for use. All the sympathy cards are still on display, as is the Valentines card that I bought her three weeks after her death.

I have found this a great comfort but notice my feelings beginning to change. Sometimes now I look at something and shudder. It brings back too many memories. It's only a matter of time before I am compelled to remove some of these items from sight.

For the moment I cope by following little rituals which have unconsciously developed: talking to Louise while walking the dog, kissing her woolly hat left by the front door each time that I go in and out and at regular intervals in-between, hugging the bannisters where I last saw her whenever I am most distressed.

And I work incessantly to memorialise her, to capture our relationship for posterity; writing my diary and these words, creating photobooks, hunting desperately for lost video clips, writing the various obituaries that are falling to me for one diverse publication or another, printing out copies of our texts and emails and all Louise's letters and other significant documents, researching information for the establishment of her charity. I won't rest, or be able to feel as though I can lift my head and properly begin to look forward, until this task is completed.

Two whole months without you Louise. It's really time that you came home now Sweetheart. I love you and I'm missing you so very much.

Why?

27th March | 63 days

I try very hard not to ask why Louise took her life. There is no need. I know why. Both the short and the long answer.

The short response is that Louise was temporarily overcome by the bleakest of darkness which she tried bravely to fight but which eventually overcame her. It subverted her ability to think rationally, to lift her head and look beyond the short-term desperation she was struggling with, to think about the consequences for myself and the rest of the family.

The longer and more complex version is probably not for here. This is the story of my journey and it's my decision to open up to that small part of the world that happens upon it. . I have to respect Louise's continuing right to privacy about the detail of her illness.

But I attended the psychiatric consultations with her and, over the years, talked to her endlessly about what she was dealing with during her intermittent episodes of depression and anxiety, even if none were quite as bleak as the last. As a reflective, intelligent and informed doctor, she was well-placed to work through and interpret her emotions and condition and to share her self-diagnosis with me.

I also have Louise's notebooks in which she was constantly writing down her thoughts, as well as a full farewell letter (something which is much less common in the case of suicide than might popularly be believed).

So I understand what was going on in Louise's mind. There is inevitably something of a gap in perception between those who have to live with mental illness and those who don't. It's impossible to properly get inside what Louise used to call her 'full head'. But I think I can get as close as it's possible for another person to do. And I know that this was something for which Louise was extremely grateful. She took enormous comfort in the thought that I understood what she was dealing with and the way it affected her.

That makes it even more difficult for me to now ask 'why?' I feel as if it's important to continue to provide Louise with this comfort. I know that the most loving thing I can say to her now is 'I'm not angry with you. I understand'. But in doing so I deny myself permission to explore the questions that continue to bewilder me and run through my mind on an almost continuous loop. The *hows* and *whys*.

I know that it wasn't Louise's settled wish to die. She loved life and when she was well, which was most of the time, she lived it with a zest, vigour and sense of joy that left others trailing in her wake. And she had the self-awareness to appreciate her good fortune too. I know that had she lived, she would now be telling me that she was so happy and so lucky to have the life that she did.

So just how could a talented, professionally-successful and relatively young woman who was physically fit, much loved, happily married and who enjoyed a good standard of living and active lifestyle, voluntarily give up everything for the sake of a handful of extremely bleak days?

How could she have got up that morning knowing that she would never see another sunrise or sunset, that she would never again hear the birdsong and smell the flowers that so enchanted her, that she would never be held, kissed or loved again, that she would never see her beloved nephews and nieces grow up into the adulthood that promises so much for them all, or that she would never feel the sun, wind or rain on her face again? How could she give up all this for... what?

Louise didn't know. Despite her faith she never held strong views on the existence or otherwise of the afterlife. Perhaps it was the scientist in her. When pressed during our lengthy philosophical conversations on long car journeys, or while preparing the Sunday roast together, the most she might venture was a vision of heaven in this life, on earth. So how could she willingly subject herself to the unknown?

I also struggle, of course, with the way that Louise was able to bring herself to do something with such horrendous implications for me and the rest of her family. How could she subject those she loved most to the cruellest of experiences imaginable? Why didn't she pick up the phone and call me, to reach out for help? Why didn't she see that she just had to hold on for a few hours, or days... that the darkness would pass and a much brighter future was just round the corner? And why, of all methods, did she have to choose that one? How could she have... at this point my mind has to close down for the sake of my own sanity.

All these questions confound me. They are beyond my comprehension. My head spins when I pose them. I want to scream them out loud. Occasionally I do. And yet, to return full circle, I know that there is no point. Because I know both Louise's considered self-diagnosis and that of her psychiatrist. I know why she chose that method of suicide. I know which fears and concerns were driving her thoughts and I also know that the darkness which sprang from them trumps everything. It wildly exaggerates and distorts problems, obscures or denies solutions, extinguishes hope. It makes the irrational appear logical and exerts an utterly irresistible destructive power.

I understand, Sweetheart. I truly do.

Falling in Love All Over Again

1st April | 68 days

I expected bereavement to bring strong emotion. Loss, guilt, anger, despair, fear. But I've realised that the strongest of all is love. When I cry out in my pain to Louise, occasionally it's to say 'Why did you do it?' or 'Why didn't you call me?' Sometimes it's to say 'I miss you', but mostly it's simply to say, over and over again, 'I love you'. It's this that I urgently want her to know now, more than anything.

I have fallen in love with Louise all over again. Of course, I had never fallen out of love with her but inevitably over four-and-a-half years together the intensity of feeling becomes more settled, comfortable and secure than in the early days of passion and discovery.

Now, however, in my reflection over what has been lost I can see more clearly than ever what it was about Louise that made her so attractive to me and what made us work so well as a couple; her wisdom, intelligence, humility, energy, compassion, beauty, enthusiastic love of life, nature and people. Her emotional intelligence and honesty, impish sense of fun, generosity of spirit, open-mindedness, desire for learning and understanding. Her values of sufficiency, toleration and giving, her bravery in fighting her illness and, of course, her reciprocal love of me.

As a consequence, my love for Louise has been redoubled. It has all the stomach-churning warmth and intensity of our first months together but sharpened further by a knowledge of her deeper qualities that could only be gained through years of intimacy, and by the memories, connections and shared experiences of a life lived together.

There is a clarity and purity to this love which I have never felt before, which sometimes takes me aback with its overwhelming force and its generosity. I would willingly sacrifice anything, including my own life and well-being, if only I could ensure Louise's welfare and happiness. It is the thought of her suffering and loss, not mine, which causes me the greatest hurt.

I yearn to be allowed a few minutes back together with Louise again to tell her all this. She knew and was secure in the knowledge that she was much loved. I told her that I loved her every day, as she did me. But over time such declarations can take on a slightly formulaic quality, genuinely meant but with the impact softened in the constant and predictable re-telling.

Beyond the early days, I rarely told her *exactly* how much she meant to me, and certainly never explained with a passion and an urgency what it would mean to me if she wasn't there anymore. I suppose, in the normal course of events, few people do. (Maybe they should. Every couple will experience this loss at some point, even if not usually so early in their time together.) In any case, I didn't fully appreciate it myself until I was placed in this nightmarish reality. Perhaps if I'd had the insight to explain all this clearly, it just might have given Louise sufficient strength and motivation to get through the darkest moment of all, though I know, deep down, that is unlikely. The depths of depression are beyond the reach of fine sentiments and rationality.

I am aware that there must be a risk of sanctifying Louise, of well-intentioned but false memory in the emotion of the moment, romanticising what she was and what we had. But whereas many people talk of 'forgetting' or a fear of 'forgetting' the person they have lost, I think that I still have a very strong sense of the real Louise, one which is grounded in reality.

I haven't lost sight of the difficult times, when she was struggling with her illness, but I know that they were an aberration and not remotely representative of the wonderful woman I knew so well. And if I was ever in any doubt, I also have the evidence of the heartfelt tributes from Louise's legion of friends who so loudly and eloquently bear witness to her remarkable qualities.

I wish I could claim that the experience of this intense love is joyful, uplifting and consolatory. After all, we are accustomed to thinking of love as a rewarding and positive emotion. Maybe it will become so again in time, when some of the raw immediacy of the hurt fades and I can remember without also mourning.

But for the moment, as I know with certainty that my love for Louise will in future be unrequited, it is simply a new and terrible form of pain and loss. What do I do with a heart full of love when it has nowhere to go?

Feeling Bad About Feeling Good

5th April | 72 days

I've been wondering what kind of person I am; self-critically examining my response to Louise's death and the way in which I am mourning. In the last few days I have generally been calmer. There have been moments in each day when I have keenly felt Louise's loss and the tears have flowed. Just seeing a couple kissing in the street was enough to cause me to break down there and then, prompting me to rush for the nearest cover to hide my tears from passers-by. But outside of these moments I am relatively emotionally stable.

It's not as if I'm not thinking about Louise the rest of the time, that somehow everything is magically better. Louise remains on my mind almost the entire day and the vast majority of my waking time is still spent talking, thinking and writing about her. This makes me sad and wistful but often without a great deal of raw distress and high emotion. I am functioning relatively normally other than for the lethargy which continues to weigh me down. Increasingly, I find myself slightly puzzled by the shock and sympathy expressed by those who I talk to for the first time since Louise's death. I find it difficult to understand why it is warranted.

So why is this? I spend hours online reading about others' experience of bereavement, absorbed in a small community unseen by the rest of the world which is brought together by the commonality of loss and grief. I know that comparisons between individuals are unhelpful, that no sure timeline can be plotted through the stages of bereavement, that our ability to cope fluctuates wildly from day-to-day and week-to-week. But I can't help wondering why, at this particular point ten weeks on, many people seem to be experiencing emotions much more sharply than I am.

Objectively I should be pleased, congratulating myself on my resilience and relieved that I am not experiencing worse. But it actually troubles me greatly. I actively *want* to grieve, *need* to grieve, in order to demonstrate to Louise the genuine depth of my love for her and the extent to which I feel her loss. I worry that if I do not, she might mistake my apparent ability to cope with day-to-day life with indifference towards her, lack of love and concern.

That is why I find myself worrying about the first day when no tears come and am almost relieved whenever I cry. While I do not want to feel miserable – I want to see a way to a future where things seem brighter —equally I do not want to allow myself to let go of the acute sense of loss and grief. It continues to bind me to Louise as strongly as we were connected in life. It is a precious emotional link which I do not want severed.

On one level I know that this is all irrational. That Louise, always an extremely acute observer of human nature, would understand better than most that grief is not measured by tears alone, and that textbook responses to bereavement are not the only proof of love. She has no wish to see me suffer and would be delighted if I adjusted rapidly to her loss and was able to achieve some kind of equilibrium. I know too that my emotional ties to her will always remain. As time goes by, they will simply be reframed in more positive terms. Grief and tears were not what brought us together as a couple or held us together and I will eventually find new and more appropriate ways of connecting with her memory.

But despite this insight I can't help thinking critically about the way I sometimes feel and behave. It is impossible to avoid feeling guilty and ashamed about every moment when I seem to find myself able to live life without Louise.

In those moments when I feel as though I am coping well, I ask myself if I am unfeeling, if I don't care. If I didn't really love Louise. Has everything I have said and done about her been false testimony, perhaps unconsciously designed to meet societal expectations of the bereaved partner? Even at my most self-critical I can see that is utterly absurd. So why the discrepancy? Is it because those people I measure myself against are atypical in their own emotional responses? There is no reason to believe that. Is it because I'm unusually strong and resilient? People sometimes tell me that I am remarkably strong but this makes me feel a fraud. They don't see me when the front door closes and I break down. I don't feel strong then.

I think that there are two explanations. The first is that I have normalised the experience of the past ten weeks in order to better cope with it. It happened, it's part of my reality so I know no different now. Doesn't everybody find their partner dead in such circumstances after only a relatively short time together?

I genuinely find it difficult to understand how it can be when I meet a couple who have been together for 20 years (20 whole years together!) or I come across a husband whose wife is much beyond the age of 40 – surely they are incredibly lucky, *they* are the exceptions, not Louise and I. Nobody sees themselves as being outside the normal experience, or a vulnerable victim of tragedy. It's not a nice place to be. Surrounding myself with people who have experienced similar loss and at a similar age also helps to reinforce the comforting impression in my mind that these things are not so unusual. This accounts for my inability to grasp why people are shocked at events.

But the second, and larger, truth is simply that I cannot absorb what has happened. Either that Louise has died or the way that she died. Whenever I think back to that night, the moments spent frantically trying to get into the house, entering through the conservatory just *knowing* for certain that I was going to see Louise hanging from the bannisters, trying to steel myself for the sight, and the desperate sometimes hysterical time afterwards with the paramedics and police, it all seems utterly unreal. I can recall every moment but almost as if it were an out-of-body experience, or as if I was watching it all on video. It just didn't really happen to me. And neither have the past 10 weeks. The self-protective layer of disbelief is still as strong as ever and it is only when it is pierced that the sheer enormity and tragedy of what has happened hits me.

I know that I keep returning to this theme but it is the most consistent of my experience of bereavement. I still struggle to grasp that somebody so close to me, so full of life, can be dead. How can it be when I see Louise's face looking back at me so alive and happy in photos every day, when her glasses are still on the kitchen worktop, when her clothes are still folded on the back of the chair in our bedroom, when her mobile phone is still next to the stereo unit, when notes in her handwriting are still stuck to the fridge door?

Death happens to the old, the physically ill, the victims of disasters and wars overseas. To others. Not to my Louise. The transition from one state to another, from life to death, may take an instant but for those left behind it seems that it takes a whole lifetime to understand. Ten weeks on, I am still numbed. If I could really grasp that I will never see Louise again, I would be in pieces all the time. Even as I write this I am unable to get my head around the concept. It's not that I am in denial. I can accept what has happened on a theoretical level. It's simply that I am unable to comprehend the consequences.

POSTSCRIPT

When I wrote this last night I was feeling strong and resilient and guilty for doing so. But today, ironically, I woke up in a completely different place. Scared, lonely, tearful, exhausted. It's a lovely sunny Easter Sunday and in normal circumstances we would have been out visiting family or friends or doing something together outdoors. Loving life and each other. Instead, I have found it difficult even to get out of bed, paralysed by my grief. I certainly have no reason today to worry about doing 'too well'. It illustrates the unpredictable, apparently arbitrary way in which these moods can sweep across me, often catching me unawares.

Both the ups and the downs are equally authentic responses to the position I find myself in. Opposite but freely interchangeable. And they both lead me to question myself. I wrote, above, that it is impossible not to feel guilty and ashamed about every moment when I seem to find myself able to live life without Louise. That is true. But then I feel equally guilty and ashamed when my distress and emotion catches up with me to the extent that it disables me. I worry about what Louise would think of me then too. But in this case, it's because I fear she would be sad at my weakness rather than my strength. It seems as though my overactive mind won't let me have any peace at present.

Life and Fate

9th April | 76 days

I should be in work by this time of the morning. Instead, I'm sitting in our bedroom crying and feeling bitter at the unfairness of it all, that I should be wrenched away from my wife who I loved so very much, and a life that I loved so very much, and handed instead a lifetime sentence of sadness, a burden of grief and loss that may in time lose some of its rawness but will remain with me to the day that I myself die.

I am not bitter towards Louise. I could never be that. I cannot blame her for her illness, she fought it so bravely and I love her from the bottom of my heart as I know she loved me. I'm just bitter that fate has singled both Louise and me out for such treatment and don't understand what either of us has done to deserve it.

Living with Uncertainty

12th April | 79 days

The night that Louise died, about the only thing that I grasped straightaway was that my life had just been turned upside down. Nothing would ever be the same again. All the certainties were gone.

I had spent years uncertain of my future, always waiting and hoping at any moment to meet the right woman, somebody with whom I could settle down for the rest of my life. That, and only that, would determine where I lived and how I lived the rest of my days.

With Louise, I had found that certainty and the security that goes with it. It wasn't as if we had elaborately-designed long-term plans but the framework was in place and the detail would look after itself. I knew that we were going to spend the rest of our lives in the house we had bought together, settling into the area and community to make it our own. I knew roughly what our financial position was likely to be as the years progressed and when semi-retirement might be feasible. I knew who I would be living my life with, the family that I would be part of, and what kind of lifestyle I would have. I knew the types of holidays we would have, the plays we would see, the type of activities we would do together, who our friends would be. I knew because it would be more of the same.

Of course, I didn't really explicitly think in those terms, or rarely so. You only tend to think about what the future holds when it can no longer be taken for granted. But unconsciously I had the security, for the first time, of knowing what my life would be and could take confidence and purpose from it. Over time, our individual lives had slowly merged together and after four-and-a-half years (it's indicative of what a short time we had together that I always include the half year) we had developed a joint existence, a merged identity. After a lot of hard work, we were beginning to establish a common past and looking forward to a common future. We revelled in that oneness.

And then that common future crumbled in the split-second it took me to see the unusual way the lights had been left on as I approached the house that January evening and knew, as a consequence, exactly what had happened.

At that point, everything that I thought I knew disappeared. My long-term horizon shrunk from decades to minutes. Far from planning a home for the rest of my life I didn't even know where I would be staying in the coming days, what those days would look like, who I would spend them with, or how I would get through them.

More than two months on there is at least some semblance of short-term structure. I'm feeling comfortable enough around the house to be able to think of staying here for the time being. In fact, at the moment, it's so important for me to be surrounded by the home we built together, which represents that common past, that it would take a crowbar to loosen my grip on it. I'm back at work and have a few entries in my social diary over the next few weeks. I have an offer of a holiday with some of Louise's relatives in the summer. It's a start.

But the medium- to long-term future is completely unresolved. I can make no assumptions about where I will be, what I will be doing, who, if anybody, I will be with and what the shape, pace and texture of my life will be. People advise me not to look too far forward, that things will resolve themselves over time. Of course they are right but I can't help myself. I am walking through a wilderness and I need to be able to lift my head and see something in the future that makes this journey worthwhile, to give me hope and inspiration.

But right now nothing is settled. I don't know how long I will be comfortable living in my house, how quickly it might turn from comforting sanctuary into a silent, stark reminder. As if to prevent myself from getting too confident, I spent one evening recently suddenly petrified of the prospect of flashbacks and visions, terrified to move in my own home. It was just one evening but many more like that and things would become untenable. It was a glimpse into what things could be like.

I've no idea at this stage how I will adapt to being on my own. Up until now the quiet evenings alone have not been so bad. I've always quite enjoyed my own company and I've tried to treat every evening in isolation, pretending that it's no different to those occasional evenings when Louise was out and I found pleasure in pottering about on my own. But it's already becoming wearing, day-after-day, closing the front door when I get home from work and knowing that I won't see anybody again until the following morning. So how will I adapt? Will I flourish as a singleton, maintain sensible routines, develop new hobbies and interests, find myself joining groups and activities, broaden my horizons and experiences? Or will I sink, lose the discipline of structure and withdraw into myself?

Not only do I not know what I will be doing, I don't know who I will be doing it with. I think and hope that I will always remain a part of Louise's family. Relationships were always good and have been further strengthened as we have tried to face these last couple of months together. I am very grateful for their support and the most practical way in which I can now help Louise is to stand – in turn – by her family, especially our nephews and nieces who represent a precious genetic link to her. I became their Uncle when I met Louise and will always remain so.

But will I be able to maintain contact with Louise's friends? I very much hope so. Not only are they rewarding people to know in their own right, but they also represent a valuable link to her, particularly those who go back many years into her student and school days. I may not be able to build new memories of Louise going forward but perhaps I can create new ones by reaching back into her past, before I met her, to live those times with her vicariously through the recollections of her friends.

And then there is possibly the biggest unknown of all. Will I eventually meet anybody else? I yearn desperately to do so one day and yet also recoil from the thought in horror. The only real balm I can think of, to soothe my pain, is to find a new relationship in time, to know again what it is like to love and be loved, to experience the simple pleasure of coming home from work to somebody who cares about me and allows me to care about them. Louise, in her farewell letter, willed me to do so, which should mean that I can think in these terms without guilt.

But of course I can't. I am currently no more ready or able to betray my love for Louise by forming a relationship with another woman than I would have been had she still been alive. Louise is still my wife and always will be. I never for one moment wanted or needed another woman. The thought of sharing my home and bed with somebody else, or removing my wedding ring, repels me. Nobody, at present, would be able to bear comparison with Louise and I could not currently conceive of a relationship which looked and felt different from the one I have valued so much.

But the human heart has an infinite capacity for love and I have to hold on to the thought that at some indeterminate point in the future I will be able to move on from this, reconcile my continuing love for Louise with love for another, and be in a place where I can recognise somebody for their own unique virtues, not how closely they can resemble Louise.

If I am then lucky enough to find the right person, somebody who will allow me to continue to openly hold and honour Louise, I am immediately propelled into a whole new world in an unknown location with unknown family and an unknown lifestyle.

Having long since accepted that my life would be without children, and become accustomed to both the welcome freedoms and the emptiness which that brings, I may find that this new world changes even those certainties and completely reframes my understanding of what a relationship looks like. I am slowly and sadly beginning to understand that even if I do meet somebody else, it will still be impossible to recreate what I once had with Louise. Things may be just as good in their own terms but they can never be the same.

I have a blank canvas, the opportunity to remake myself. But I don't want it. I spent years adapting myself to fit the relationship with Louise. It was hard work at times, stretching and challenging me to develop in all sorts of positive ways I could never have foreseen. I did it successfully and loved the rewards it brought but I do not currently have the energy to start all over again. So the future opens up in front of me: cold, frightening, uninviting, unknown. It's an odd feeling for somebody in their mid-40's who should be, and was, settled in life. I have almost no structure to cling onto and don't know where I am headed. I will find a way but I haven't a clue where it will lead me.

Spring Blues

17th April | 84 days

It's 12 weeks today since Louise died. I've stopped counting the individual days but the number of weeks which have passed still comes to me as naturally as breathing. It's become a mark of my identity.

I'm not alone. I've noticed that whenever people who are recently widowed gather together in support groups, whether online or in the real world, the passage of time since the loss of our partners is one of our first self-descriptors, handy shorthand for the condition we currently find ourselves in, not dissimilar to women in pregnancy. 'I'm at 6/10/12/15 weeks' is often enough to tell others much about our current mental state and ability to deal with the world.

And while all our journeys are different, many people further down the path than myself will highlight the three-month mark as perhaps the lowest point. I didn't quite get this initially. How could anything be worse than the blood-red raw pain and despair in the immediate aftermath of loss? Well of course it's not, but it *is* a different kind of low. I'm now close enough to the marker to be feeling the same effects and I see the truth in it. Just when I thought, at 10 or so weeks, that I was gaining some kind of control over the situation, the last week has been my toughest since the very early days. There has been more emotion, more tears and a heavier overlay of sadness than I have experienced for some time.

I have been more vulnerable to the slightest trigger. Seeing an advert on TV showing a couple journeying through the stages of life together after successfully applying for a mortgage was enough to induce a 15-minute breakdown. Finding the (still unwritten) Valentine's card Louise had bought for me before her death, tucked away safely in her bedside cabinet drawer, left me gasping for breath for a couple of days.

After surviving the first couple of weeks back at work without any major breakdowns, almost every day in the last week has seen me rush for the privacy of an empty meeting room, or failing that a toilet cubicle, so that I can sob my heart out without alerting the rest of the office. I feel enough of a freak as it is, the person everybody is talking about in hushed tones, without breaking down in front of all my colleagues. But I need to be quick because I usually only have a few seconds warning of what is about to overtake me.

I shouldn't need to ask myself why things are tougher at the moment. I should just accept it and save what little energy I have for getting through. But I'm not Louise's husband for nothing (the present tense will always apply) and, just as she would, I need to analyse why this is a more difficult period.

I'm sure it's largely due to the fact that the shock is subsiding and the numbness and disbelief which have acted as my protective shell are therefore beginning to wear off. My brain has allowed itself to begin to process the new reality. The sheer passage of time for which Louise has been absent forces me to begin to accept that she isn't coming back. Things feel more real than they did a few weeks ago. More than ever before, I find memories and thoughts of Louise are instantly accompanied by the crushing thought that we will never again do whatever it was I was fondly remembering, whereas previously that same thought was too incomprehensible to absorb.

And at the very same time as I am struggling to deal with this new more exposed and vulnerable self, the external support dwindles as friends inevitably and properly return to their own lives. That's not intended as a criticism. It happens in every case at this stage. It would be impossible to maintain those initial levels of support and, frankly, I wouldn't have the energy to respond to such a volume of emails, texts and phone calls anyway. I don't like Facebook at the best of times but find it even more difficult than usual at present, seeing the news streams from friends fill up once more with photos of family, jokes and political comment. Life for others resumes. It has to. I understand that. But it can't for me.

There is, however, another factor at present. Spring. The recent sunny and mild weather has been difficult for me to deal with. Like most people, Louise loved this time of year. I recall a text from her sent to me at work during a period in December when she was struggling. She told me that she had been planting daffodils in the garden and she was 'looking forward to Spring'. Every morning when I get up I now see those daffodils, and the tulips with which our garden is also ablaze, and it breaks my heart afresh that Louise hasn't got to see them, nor ever will again. I can feel the general uplift in people's spirits out on the streets and feel utterly disconnected from it; alienated by it. Even the bird song seems to mock the fact that Louise will no longer be able to hear it. I was going to get the garden furniture out of its winter hibernation when temperatures soared the other day but didn't have the heart. I just couldn't bring myself to get only one chair out of the shed.

With every sunny day, I find myself wondering what Louise and I would have been doing had things been different. Maybe we would have visited family and friends, or gone on a bike ride. Perhaps we would have played tennis or gone to a National Trust property, or been for a stroll on Louise's beloved South Bank.

Whatever we would have been doing, I most certainly wouldn't have been lying in bed until lunchtime on a weekend, trying to summon up the courage and the energy to start another day and hating myself for my lethargy and lack of structure. Spring somehow brings the contrast between what was and what is into ever-sharper focus. At the moment, I wish it was Autumn. Maybe by then I will be counting in months rather than weeks.

Crying Time

23rd April | 90 days

I've now cried on 90 consecutive days. I never imagined that I would come to know the experience of crying so intimately, to recognise so well the sensation, the distinctive noise, the smell and the taste of the tears themselves and the stinging and burning aftermath in my eyes. All now are as familiar to me as breathing.

I've almost come to welcome the tears as a release and a sign of my love for Louise. Moments of honesty when I can put aside the outward pretence and just surrender to my inner voice crying out in pain. I wake up every day knowing that the tears will come. I just don't know when or whether it will be a flood or a trickle. There is no pattern and no apparent reason why some days should be more emotional than others. Every time I think that I've reached the point where the tears are drying up I find myself knocked sideways again.

Most people around me wouldn't know any of this. I still try and hide my tears from others. Although it has become routine to me, I know that it makes them uncomfortable. They want to help. But in truth I don't need anybody with me when I cry. There is no consolation that can be given, nothing that can be done. Nobody can bring Louise back so I might as well cry alone. At least that way I can be as uninhibited, as distressed and, occasionally, as angry as I need to be without causing embarrassment to myself or others.

If truth be told, I don't really want the tears to stop. They somehow represent an emotional connection with Louise, proof that I continue to feel for her in the present. She may be dead but my love for her is still very much alive. It's better to feel grief than nothing at all.

Piercing My Soul

Since Louse's death, my laptop has barely left my side. It has become my constant travelling companion. Even when away from home it has been the first thing that I have packed.

I have long since discovered that the only effective balm that can be applied to my wounds when they are at their most raw is writing about them. Whenever my emotions overwhelm me, therefore, I reach for my laptop and write. Indeed it is the very reason for the existence of this book. Somehow the discipline and structure that writing requires of me helps both to process my thoughts and to calm me. And this evening, sitting in a hotel room in Stockport after a family wedding party, I really needed to be calmed.

No doubt the hotel reception staff thought that they were doing me a favour when they upgraded me from a single room to a double. They were wrong. Hotels used to signify holidays, happy times spent with Louise. But I suddenly found myself in a double room on my own, remembering all that has gone before and been lost. Worse, much worse, I briefly allowed my mind to stray into areas I normally manage to keep firmly locked, the very darkest of places; the moments Louise experienced after she kicked the stool away.

I try to be as open and honest as possible in my writing. It's therapeutic to confront my innermost thoughts in this way and I hope that in doing so I can somehow help others struggling unsteadily down a similar path. But here I have to exercise discretion. I can't tell you what I imagined, the scene I pictured of Louise's final struggle. It's not fair on me to have to imagine it and it's not fair on anybody reading it to share that vision.

I really have no adequate words for the impact of my imaginings. They pierce my soul. It creates a sense of helplessness, torment and despair – like no other – to think of the person I love so much, with whom I had shared so much, and who I wanted to support, protect and nurture, in the dark, on her own, struggling and suffering in the cruellest possible way. My greatest fear of all is that in the moment she had changed her mind and no longer wanted to die, but too late to do anything to save herself.

I keep on re-imagining that evening, creating scenarios in my mind where I get home from work in time to save Louise, holding her up, literally and figuratively, allowing her to breathe until help arrived. Somehow that only makes things worse, allowing me almost to believe that there was a very different and much happier outcome.

Every time that I look at a photo of Louise laughing, smiling, loving life, I cannot help but think of the way she was when I found her and how she got to that point. From a selfish perspective, it's as if the happiest years of my life have been taken away from me… expunged. The wonderful memories which I thought were mine – forever wrecked by what was to come. But far, far worse is the knowledge of what Louise herself suffered.

I'm assured that I'm dealing with all of these issues well. The Clinical Psychologist to whom I was referred, for reasons which neither of us could quite understand, instead of bereavement counselling, quickly told me that she had no grounds to continue to see me because I was 'coping remarkably well in the circumstances'.

Maybe I am. But however strong I may appear to others, and however normally I may apparently continue to function, it doesn't make the pain go away and it won't prevent me carrying that same pain for the rest of my life.

Humbled

30th April | 97 days

After four-and-a-half years together, and three months since her death, I thought that I knew everything there was to know about Louise. But this afternoon I discovered another aspect of her life which I had previously only briefly glimpsed.

I am sitting here perhaps at my very lowest point yet, emotionally and physically exhausted. My stomach is still churning many hours after a beautiful yet traumatic Memorial Service held by Louise's Practice to celebrate her life as a doctor. It took me back nearly three months to the main Service of Remembrance, but then I was still wrapped in my protective bubble of shock and numbness, mechanically going through the motions, barely knowing what was happening to me or around me. Back then I didn't fully appreciate that I was broken, or at least what it felt like to be broken.

Now things are very different. The numbness has gone and the grim reality of daily life without Louise has set in. I know that I won't see her, hear her or touch her again, at least in this existence and I am beginning to understand what it is like to live within that void. I am also now exhausted by three months of mourning, a process infinitely more intense and all-consuming than anything else I have ever experienced. I have no emotional or physical reserves of strength or energy left to call upon.

Today's Service was therefore very much harder to cope with. To sit through a Memorial Service for the person you love so much is simultaneously an excruciating, surreal and uplifting experience which strips bare your personal life and emotions and exposes them to the gaze of countless others.

To self-consciously enter a church filled with hundreds of people knowing that all eyes are upon you, that you are the object of the collective sympathy of so many – most of whom you don't know, or know only barely – is only the beginning of the challenge. You then have to sit and stare at a big screen which bewilderingly declares that this is the Memorial Service of your beloved wife and displays a photo of her at her most beautiful, before listening to speaker after speaker paying tribute to her, and then to watch slide shows of your own personal photos of her, precious memories of holidays and family events, playing to a soundtrack of music of deep personal resonance and meaning.

And then, after fighting so hard to maintain your composure, to avoid eye contact with anybody lest everything falls apart, comes the hardest test of all. The moment when you have to step forward and deliver your own eulogy, desperate to be coherent and to do your wife proud, but conscious that every word is a potential trip hazard; that a full scale and very public meltdown into floods of tears is possible at any moment.

But the reward for enduring this agony was to gain an insight into the one aspect of Louise's life which I couldn't normally experience alongside her. Always mindful of the need for patient confidentiality, Louise told me relatively little about the detail of her working day but she did frequently voice her frustrations at her own perceived professional limitations and we frequently tried to work through this self-doubt together. I knew that Louise must be a better doctor than she gave herself credit for, and the occasional comment from patients which filtered through to me hinted at her very special gifts but, being neither her colleague nor her patient, I could hardly provide an objective assessment.

It was therefore a privilege today to meet Louise's patients and colleagues and to understand that Louise was not just a good doctor but a truly outstanding one. I learnt how highly regarded she was within the Practice and the wider medical community and how loved she was by her patients for the care and commitment she displayed towards them. I was overwhelmed reading the book of condolences in which patient after patient describes with enormous gratitude the lengths Louise went to in order to support them and the difference that she was able to make to their lives. It was humbling to know that my wife, the person who I saw close up in all her daily vulnerability and humanity, was held in such remarkable affection and had been able to change so many people's lives for the better, and to do so in her own quiet and unassuming way.

And yet even here, amongst the pride, there was profound sadness. For every tribute, every acknowledgement of Louise's extraordinary gifts and personality, there was another painfully sharp reminder of what has been lost, not only by her patients but also by me.

I have tried to console myself with the thought that one day in the distant future I may be ready to love again, to try and recreate with somebody else something of what I had with Louise. But days like today only serve to emphasise yet again what I already knew; that Louise was a person of such outstanding character, so full of the most extraordinary energy, love, commitment, intelligence, wisdom, fun and goodness that it is quite impossible to ever hope to meet anybody of her like again.

I have been lucky enough to have the very best and unlucky enough to have lost it. The rest of my life can therefore now be nothing more than a search for second best.

Resisting the Domino Effect

2nd May | 99 days

There is often panicked talk in the media about suicide clusters. This usually concentrates on young people and the possibility of copycat deaths, vulnerable and depressed teenagers following the example set by a peer to take a way out.

But the contagion of suicide can also manifest itself when the intensity of despair over the loss of a loved one leads a member of their family, or a friend, to take the same course of action themselves shortly afterwards. Only today I learned of such a case locally and Louise herself took her life just three months after her father did the same, although with Louise the relationship between the two incidents was a little less direct. Her father's death didn't make her own inevitable, but it created the conditions in which it became possible.

It is easy to see how there can be a domino effect. I have always been clear that in this case that stops with me. There will be no more suicides no matter how bleak, how hopeless things may appear. I am not mentally ill, I am grieving. Many of the symptoms may be superficially similar but there are some crucial differences; my head is clear enough to enable me to retain an appreciation of the broader context and the consequences for my family, I can understand that although life is currently more miserable than I could ever have conceived, time will eventually bring at least some respite.

And, perhaps most crucially, because I am not ill I retain responsibility for my actions. Louise always bravely accepted responsibility for everything she said and did whilst she was ill but she should not have tried to carry that burden. Nobody would expect a cancer sufferer to be responsible for the course of their illness so it would be entirely wrong to hold Louise to account for anything which she did in the midst of hers.

But it's true that there have been occasions in recent days and weeks when I have seen some attraction in the idea. Not because I don't love and appreciate life. On the contrary. Having experienced its shocking fragility and felt my heart bleed for what Louise has lost, her inability to any longer enjoy the simple pleasures and joys of life, I understand more than ever the precious nature of the gift of life and the need to embrace it and revel in it.

Nevertheless, my deep yearning for Louise, my love for her, the emptiness in my heart and my sense of hopelessness about a future without her are so overwhelming that I can't help but think that anything which speeds up the time to when we are reunited in heaven, if such a place exists, must be positive.

Louise was by far the best thing that ever happened to me, the most beautiful person, inside and out, that I have ever met. As a couple we complemented each other perfectly, our values, tastes and outlook on life, and the way we wanted to treat our partner and be treated by them were almost an exact match. We were more than the sum of our parts – where one was weak the other was strong and vice versa. As time went by our love was growing even stronger and our relationship even more fulfilling. I cannot conceive of a positive future without Louise and dread the broken life ahead of me. I vividly recall, just days after her death, standing waiting to cross a busy road and for a split-second thinking how easy it would be to walk in front of the oncoming bus.

However, nobody need worry about me. I must be clear; suicide is almost never the right option and it certainly isn't a remotely sensible course of action for me. To begin with, I'm not nearly as brave as Louise. It wouldn't have been easy to walk in front of that bus at all, to completely disregard every natural survival instinct hardwired into me.

But in any case, one of the reasons why Louise took her life was because in the muddled thinking of the moment of depression she genuinely thought that her death would release me to live a better life, free from worry and anxiety about her and the challenge presented by her mental health issues. She certainly didn't want me to follow her so soon. If nothing else, it therefore means that I am obliged to try to live the best life that I can, otherwise her sacrifice will somehow seem to be even more senseless and wasteful than it already is. In time, when I am stronger, I will attempt to do that. I don't presently have any motivation for my own needs but if I can make Louise happy it will be worth it.

Cutting Through the Grief

5th May | 102 days

Today was a numb day. That's good because disbelief and not feeling is better than the alternative of understanding and despair. And it's especially good because it was a Bank Holiday, and I have already found them to be difficult days to navigate – everybody appears to be out and about enjoying themselves whereas my day is empty and I can't stop thinking about what Louise and I would be doing in normal circumstances. I resent the holiday mood because it jars so much with my own.

I'm hoping that after several weeks of real struggle it marks some sort of upswing. Not permanent progress of course. Grief is not linear. While the classical model of the five stages of grief might sound as though there is some form of neatly packaged chronology of progression, the emotions are actually experienced in a much more fluid, almost chaotic way. Rather than a straight road, the journey through bereavement is more like a maze. You constantly go backwards and forwards, round and about, doubling up on yourself. Sometimes you think that you are close to finding the exit but it's always an illusion and without warning you quickly find that you are hopelessly lost again.

Nevertheless, a temporary anaesthetic is better than none at all, so feeling slightly more capable than in recent days, I decided to tackle the garden, which has lain untouched since Louise died. It's nothing particularly grand, just an ordinary suburban back garden of the type found in thousands of inter-war semis and terraced houses. But it's reasonably quiet and secluded and a vast improvement on the cramped back yard we previously had in a central London ground floor flat. It was one of the main reasons we bought the house.

While I enjoy having a nice garden I'm not one of nature's gardeners. It was very much Louise's domain. It wasn't so much that Louise was an expert either, but, as with most things in life, whereas I planned, Louise did, and enjoyed doing. I haven't got a clue how the garden works and will have to take advice on that at some point – it's one of those many domestic puzzles that I'm going to need to try and figure out now. I want to maintain it for Louise's sake.

But one thing that always fell to me was cutting the grass. It was simple enough for me to manage and always left me feeling good, less for the aesthetics of the garden and more because it was one of those activities that made me feel properly married. After waiting so long in my life, here I was in my own garden, cutting my own lawn while my lovely wife was indoors preparing lunch. It's a clichéd gender-driven view of domesticity which might be derided by some but at heart I'm pretty conventional and it always made me feel good; about myself, my achievements in life and my marriage. I had to wait until I was well into my 40's but at last I was finally fulfilling the suburban domestic ideal.

Mowing the lawn wasn't an easy task today though. After months of grief-induced neglect, the grass was badly overgrown and difficult to cut. My progress was slowed further as I couldn't help but keep looking back at the house, wishing that I would be able to see Louise in the kitchen or sitting in the conservatory.

The end result looked superficially respectable from a distance but it took only a cursory inspection to realise that it was all rather ragged, uneven and much of the lawn was brown, dead or dying; a pale shadow of the way it had been only a short time ago. It struck me that the state of the garden probably serves as a good metaphor for the life I am now leading. From the outside, looking in, it can appear as though there is some form of normality. I'm still standing, still just about functioning and slowly resuming some of my normal activities. But close to, it's apparent that nothing is as it was, nor will it ever be again. Everything is diminished, damaged. Just as the garden will take a lot of work even to maintain in its present state, work which I don't have the energy, knowledge or skills to properly undertake, so too will I.

POSTSCRIPT

A newly-cut lawn, however imperfect, demands garden furniture so it can be enjoyed. But how many chairs to take out of the shed? I put just the one out but am now feeling guilty. I haven't swapped the sofas for armchairs, nor have I exchanged the double bed for a single. Louise can still join me in the lounge and the bedroom. I can't exclude her from the garden. I'll put a chair out for her tomorrow.

Surviving Louise's Birthday

7th May | 104 days

The only predictable thing about grief, it seems, is its unpredictability. Yesterday would have been (or should that be 'was'?) Louise's 41st birthday. I have been steeling myself for this moment almost ever since Louise died, conscious that many of my fellow widows and widowers who form such a valuable online self-help community report significant anniversaries to be particularly difficult occasions. This was the first, and one of the most important, of those anniversaries and I expected it to be one of my biggest challenges to date. So too, it seems, did family, friends and colleagues who got in touch to wish me well in large numbers.

Yet I surprised myself with the way in which I largely managed to get through the day. Of course there was indescribable sadness, but I was calmer and more composed than I thought I might be.

I'm fortunate that numbness has returned in recent days, bringing with it an inability to comprehend what has happened. Bewilderment is back. This leaves me angry with myself for my failure to understand what should be quite simple – Louise is dead and not returning – but at the same time brings the blessing of a stunted range of emotional responses. Things which would have reduced me to floods of tears a few days ago no longer do so. A busy day at work provided some distraction as well and the tide of good wishes helped. Not only did they make me feel less isolated but they also comforted me with the thought that Louise is not forgotten.

But I was still faced with the challenge of how to mark the day. Sometimes it seems as though bereavement is nothing but a series of unwelcome dilemmas, questions both large and small, which cannot possibly have a single definitive answer but to which great emotional significance is attached. Where would Louise want her ashes scattered? Who would she want to have her various possessions? How long do I wear my wedding ring for? When should I take the sympathy cards down? Should her obituaries be in her maiden name (by which she was still known for professional purposes) or her married name? What should be the objects of Louise's Memorial Fund? Should I put pillows on her side of the bed? And so it goes on. Each and every one designed to torment as I struggle to do the right thing and find the answer that Louise would choose.

Usually, it's fairly easy to know how to celebrate your partner's birthday. Presents, a card, flowers, a nice meal out. But how do you adapt this formula when they are no longer alive? I needed in some way to recognise the occasion, to express my love for Louise. My limited imagination could come up with nothing more original than something as close as possible to the normal conventions.

The gift was relatively straightforward. Louise's 40th birthday present from me was a donation to a hostel for the homeless so it wasn't such a leap from that to a donation, in her name, to the children's play charity which we had asked people to give to in lieu of presents at the time of our wedding.

But the rest was more problematic. Sainsbury's doesn't have a great range of birthday cards for the deceased (a rare gap in the greetings card market). I could see the funny side in trying to find something with appropriate wording for somebody who died three months ago, but it was rather a struggle – anything which suggested looking forward to the future, for example, had to be out.

As all that could be done was for me to write the card and then read it out loud for Louise to hear, no envelope was necessary but I picked one up to avoid the checkout operator remarking on its absence. In fact, going through the tills caused some anxiety. I was clutching flowers and a card wishing my wife a happy birthday. I was relieved that the woman didn't ask what we were planning to do to celebrate. I didn't have a clue how I would have responded to any such innocent remark. Admission of the truth, that the person for whom I was buying these items no longer existed, would have caused embarrassment all round; I'm not sure that I'm capable of the pretence that my wife is still alive and all is normal just for the sake of social nicety.

I left the flowers at the spot where Louise's ashes were scattered. It's normally pretty quiet. On a damp, windy evening I expected to have the place to myself but instead arrived to find a photoshoot, complete with glamour model, taking place next to Louise's trees. While I arranged the flowers as best as I could, tears streaming and talking out loud to Louise, photographer and model made a hasty exit, looking back at me and whispering amongst themselves. That is what I have become. At 46 years of age I *am* that sad man alone and crying on the park bench, lost in his memories and an object of pity for others.

Somehow, there, on the park bench, I felt Louise's loss even more acutely than I usually do at home. Apart from her absence, the house still feels pretty normal. But this was a powerful statement. A year ago, we had enjoyed a large picnic with dozens of Louise's friends in the same park for her 40th birthday. Louise was very much alive, happy, vibrant, positively glowing. Now I sat there in the drizzle and evening gloom talking to a bunch of flowers laid under a tree. I'm grateful that we can't know our futures.

One consolation struck me. Although another year has passed since her birth, Louise will now never age. I looked forward very much to discovering how she would grow into first middle and then old age. One of my most precious photos of her was taken just six months ago, on holiday in Sicily. The lighting and the angle of her face gave a tantalising glimpse of the refined, almost regal, features she would have developed had she lived. It was an early indication of her transition from young woman to mature beauty, her full blossoming.

Louise herself sometimes joked about looking forward to being old so that she could, like the woman in one of her favourite poems, act outrageously and wear purple. But there was another truth behind this. Louise was scared of illness and infirmity in old age, of being a burden on others. Scared perhaps in a way that only a doctor, who has seen so much suffering, can be. She occasionally talked about the future possibility, should it be required, of assisted dying.

But now Louise will not have to cope with any of that. No matter how many birthdays pass she will never grow old. While I become decrepit, Louise will always remain as vigorous, fit and alert as she so much wanted to be. Sweetheart, I will celebrate your birthdays with you for all eternity.

Living a Lie

8th May | 105 days

People think that I'm strong, that I'm getting through. They ask me if things are a little easier now.

I can see why. I look and sound normal. I get up on a morning (usually), go to work, do the shopping. Sometimes I bring myself to talk about other things. Occasionally I smile. Once or twice I have even laughed. Sometimes I manage to fool myself. I think that I am making progress, that I can do this, that there is still a life worth living even if it is diminished. Sometimes I am even rather proud of the way in which I am managing things.

But then there are times, like this morning, when the facade crumbles. It's kept out of sight, behind my locked front door, but if people saw me then they would know that I am not strong. I am weak, lost, afraid and above all desperately lonely.

Out of nowhere, often when I am least expecting it, I'm suddenly and brutally hit by a tsunami of emotion, a great overpowering tidal wave of loss, despair, hopelessness. I am completely disabled by the raw elemental force of this grief. I desperately yearn with an intensity of longing that I have never before experienced to hold and cuddle Louise, to be able to talk to her, explain to her what it is like living this life, to apologise both for what I got wrong in her care during her last days and what I get wrong now as I try to live in a way worthy of her memory. Above all I want to tell her over and over and over again that I love her and that I miss her. I cry and cry and cry until the tears run out.

I am completely broken. I will superficially patch myself back up and carry on, if only for Louise's sake. Even as I type this the tears have stopped, my breathing is slowing and very shortly I shall open the front door to the world to go to work and resume the great act. No doubt, in time, I will learn how to better adapt to the damage, to accept it as part of me and live with it. But I can never be mended.

Learning from Louise

14th May | 111 days

As we go through life we all inevitably find ourselves marked by our experiences. We collect and carry our scars, whether they be of disappointment, disillusionment, failure, betrayal, trauma or tragedy. And these experiences in turn help to make us the person that we are, for better or worse.

If I am going to bring any kind of sense to what Louise did I have to try and find and hold on to positives that have emerged from it. Of course, nothing can provide adequate compensation or anything remotely like it. But I must be able to see some good come from her actions, however slight the consolation may be. I must believe that even the darkest act can in some way bring light and hope. Then, at least, there is some purpose and benefit. Louise will not have died completely in vain.

The most immediate and obvious positive is the way in which Louise's death has brought me closer to her family and friends. Louise's mother, brother and sister, and our nephews and nieces, were for three-and-a-half years my family by marriage. Relationships were always good but they have been strengthened further in adversity and they will now always remain family. The support I have received from some of Louise's friends has also created lifetime bonds.

But there is something more, something deeper. Louise may have been six years younger than me but she taught me much. My life and my interests became infinitely richer, more textured and varied thanks to her example, enthusiasm and encouragement. I began to look beyond the relatively narrow confines of football, photography, politics and history. As I joined with Louise in her interests, reluctantly at first but with increasing enthusiasm, I found myself eagerly perusing theatrical listings and reviews, attending classical concerts, downloading choral music, enjoying road trip holidays in VW camper vans (I drew the line at camping after a very chilly, soggy and muddy weekend in a tipi) and even appreciating long country walks.

All of this was new to me and all of it will survive Louise's passing. Curiously, in fact, since her death I seem almost to have mysteriously acquired Louise's own interests and way of relating to the world. It's as if, through some strange force, I am experiencing life for her by proxy. I find myself realising with sudden clarity exactly what it was that made Louise love nature so much. For the first time in my life I am drawn to stop and admire flowers, watch birds and stroke the bark of trees, just as Louise would. And Louise will be both amused and impressed that the man who used to think a stroll to the corner shop for a newspaper constituted a long walk has been seriously considering going on an organised walking holiday.

Of even more significance, however, Louise possessed a generosity, wisdom, grace and understanding of people way beyond mine. I have learnt so much from her about how to treat people, how to think beyond the exterior and how to always look for the beautiful – in people, in nature and in life generally. I therefore cannot afford to allow the scars from her death to diminish me as a person. The best tribute that I can pay to Louise, my best motivation for recovery and the only appropriate way to bring some meaning and purpose to what has happened, is for me to use this experience and my learning from Louise to become a better person and help the world in some small way become a better place.

We used to sometimes say to each other, "I am yours, you are mine and we are one". I'm conscious that sounds rather twee out of context but if it is to have any meaning then surely it is in these circumstances. By taking Louise's values and principles as my own, upholding and honouring them, then Louise can in some way continue to live, to make the difference to people's lives that she so much wanted, through me.

The charity which I am establishing in Louise's memory to help medical practitioners at risk of suicide, and their families, is one practical manifestation of the desire to create a positive legacy. But I am determined to effect more deep-rooted personal change, to become a better person through daily observance of Louise's values in all aspects of my life.

This will not necessarily be easy to do. Those values are good ones and close to my own but I will still have to work hard to live up to them; not to judge others, not to allow myself to feel or display anger or strong negative emotions (I never once heard Louise use the word 'hate'), to always see the positive in everybody and every situation, to always give time to listen and, perhaps most crucially, once a wrong has been identified to act rather than merely talk about it. In every situation I will have to stop and ask myself what Louise would have done. This is bound to provide me with the right course of action and a reliable moral compass.

If I can do all this then I will be able to draw some comfort from the knowledge that Louise's death was not entirely without purpose and that indirectly she will be able to continue to exert a positive influence on the world. I also very much hope that it might make her proud of me.

All My Trials, Lord

17th May | 114 days

I've been doing well this week. Fortified by numbness and that familiar sense of incomprehension and disbelief, I have at times come close to some kind of normal function. The hammering of grief in my head and heart has been reduced to a low-pitched hum, ever present but not disabling. The stream of tears has slowed to a trickle and I have been waking each morning in the near sure – if always mistaken – expectation that the coming day would be my first without crying since 23rd January.

My newfound strength led me to examine one of those potential emotional timebombs that lie in wait for me all over the house, in every drawer, under every pile of paper, in every digital archive; an Aled Jones track on my Spotify playlist which I knew must be there because Louise had listened to it. It didn't seem to quite fit with our normal musical tastes.

One glance at the title, 'All my Trials, Lord', and I knew the bomb had exploded. A quick internet search for the lyrics left me in a heap on the floor, both literally and metaphorically. Mixing metaphors, yet again, the juggernaut of grief had flattened me when I had been least expecting it. This was what Louise, during the depths of her crisis, had been listening to for comfort and, perhaps, inspiration;

All my trials, Lord
Soon be over

I had a little book that was given to me
And every page spelt liberty
All my trials
Soon be over

Too late my brothers
Too late but never mind
All my trials, Lord
Soon be over

There is a tree in paradise
That pilgrims call it the tree of life
All my trials, Lord
Soon be over

Too late my brothers
Too late
But never mind
All my trials, Lord
Soon be over
All my trials, Lord
Soon be over

I have been trying so hard, with some success, to blot out thoughts of Louise's
mental turmoil and anguish in the weeks leading up to her death. But here was
fresh, heartbreakingly eloquent evidence of the despair she was experiencing
and the only hope that she believed she had left to cling on to. It felt as though
my heart had been sliced open. If only I had noticed the track appear in the
play list at the time, it might have further alerted me to her state of mind. If, if,
if…

I have tried to use love as a form of resistance. It has its limits. All my love was
not powerful enough to save Louise. I fervently hope that her trials are indeed
over, but in the process they have become mine. And yet, as I lay crumpled
underneath the bannisters, all I had left to fall back on for comfort, yet again,
was love.

The Relief of Numbness

24th May | 121 days

'Shit, shit, shit, shit, shit, shit.'

I never swear. Ever. Well, hardly ever. I swear so infrequently that I feel incredibly self-conscious whenever I do so. When I used to read to Louise as we lay in bed, my left arm always curled around her, holding up the book in my right hand, she would be amused whenever the dialogue demanded that I use industrial language, enjoying the novelty value of hearing me utter profanities, even if they were in the voice of another. David Nicholls provided her with much more of this form of entertainment than Dickens.

And yet I find myself now sitting in my lounge involuntarily and angrily uttering this dubious one word mantra. On Friday, I had what might pass for almost a normal pleasantly sociable meal out with a friend. She remarked on how I seemed to be in a much better place than when we had last met several weeks ago. She was right.

But this weekend I'm weepy and emotional and the reality of the situation has taken hold of me again, prompting that heartfelt and, for me, remarkable, outburst. How can I go from that to this so quickly? How can such an all-consuming emotion as grief be so transient, sometimes overwhelming me with its force, sometimes bewildering me with its absence?

The answer, I think, is that it isn't. Grief is constant, enduring. What changes is the extent to which the pain of grief can be masked by nature's natural anaesthetic: numbness. The state of numbness is, by definition, difficult to describe since it is something of a void, but it disables my ability to feel or to grasp the concept of Louise's death. It has something of the character of an out-of-body experience. I can see and hear everything going on around me but cannot feel it.

When I am numb, I theoretically understand that Louise is dead, that she is never coming back, but the meaning of it doesn't truly register. I repeat to myself over and over the words 'Louise is dead, Louise is dead' to try and fill this mental lacuna, almost as if I was slapping the face of a drunk to try and rouse them, but the words are meaningless. It's not so much disbelief as incomprehension. It's an odd thing to think that I can live with a straightforward fact for four whole months yet frequently not be able to understand it.

Numbness has been my regular companion throughout this journey. Initially, I worried about its effect, thinking that there was something wrong with me, that I wasn't grieving appropriately, not showing Louise due respect and love. But over time I have learnt to recognise it for what it is, vital respite from the physically and mentally exhausting task of grieving, and to be grateful for it. Numbness provides me with the ability to function. Numbness is what others mistake for strength.

Numbness got me through those first two weeks, the period from Louise's death to her funeral, not just enabling me to get out of bed and perform basic functions such as eating and sleeping but much more demanding tasks like planning the funeral and writing and delivering my Eulogy at the Memorial Service.

Even now, under its influence, I can find myself talking matter-of-factly about the events surrounding Louise's death – the moment of breaking into the house (the front door had been locked from the inside) and finding her in the hallway – without emotion. I can see the shock, horror and pity on the face of the listener but I, the person that experienced it, feels nothing. I can concentrate, after a fashion, for seven hours a day at work, plan a holiday, live in a house surrounded by memories and reminders. I can make my dinner in the kitchen and barely ever so much as glance at the large crematorium-issue plastic jar on top of the cupboards that looks for all the world as if it holds sweets but actually contains the remnants of Louise's ashes which I intend to scatter in the garden when it is looking more respectable.

While I am numb, none of this is particularly difficult. It's when the anaesthetic wears off that I cannot cope, when despair and sadness reassert their grip. It usually happens without notice. I find myself sitting quietly on the sofa or in the car and am suddenly jolted by an electric current of a thought. 'Louise is dead'. And this time it registers. The raw and bleeding wound that is grief is exposed once again. I understand what it means, for her, for me, for us. The finality.

'Shit, shit, shit, shit, shit, shit.'

Faith, Hope and the Unknown

28th May | 125 days

Whenever I am asked to identify my faith for official purposes, I always hesitate over the box labelled 'Agnostic' before eventually ticking the one marked 'Christian'.

Of course, to describe myself as Christian is anything but a simple and unambiguous statement because its interpretation will vary enormously depending upon the faith, or lack thereof, of each individual. I should therefore be clear that I do not come from the same Christian tradition as Louise, one where belief and worship and the word of scripture are not just central to life but the very meaning *for* life. I respect it but I am not part of it.

Insofar as I have ever thought about it, and until I met Louise I rarely did, my Christianity has been based on hope rather than certainty. It might best be described as a form of secularised Christianity which reflects the values of the contemporary western liberal society in which I have been brought up. I have never read the Bible and, again until I met Louise, had never attended any form of church worship.

I have been ignorant of church traditions and thought, beyond the broadest of themes which manage to seep into the secular consciousness. I am instinctively uncomfortable with spiritual certainty, unable to reconcile this with the diversity of thought and belief which I know to exist and the sheer improbability of one group, one society, one culture, having a monopoly on truth and wisdom. Brought up to challenge and look for evidential standards of proof of some form of guiding hand, I have found nothing.

Nevertheless, I have always held on to a vague spirituality. My hope has been largely based both on a selfish need to comfort myself with the prospect of something more beyond this life and a rather more altruistic desire for a settled order of things in which goodness, love and justice prevail in a way in which they so clearly do not in this domain.

So I have believed – or very much tried to believe – in a greater force for goodness. Call Him, Her, or It, God if you will. My God, to whom I have always prayed every day, very much reflects my own values, or at least those to which I aspire – inclusive, tolerant, forgiving, capable of infinite love and understanding. As I happen to have been brought up in a society of Christian tradition I have naturally framed this within a broadly Christian context, appropriating those parts of the Biblical message which seem to me to be right and proper and discarding those aspects which are inconsistent with my construct. It's a convenient and probably lazy consumerist pick-and-mix approach.

In recent years, as Louise challenged her faith and evolved her thinking, we promised ourselves that we would explore the Quaker movement. We read a little about the specifically British tradition of Quaker thought and practice and attended a couple of Meetings for Worship when visiting a friend who is a 'Friend'. We were attracted by the gentleness, the stillness, the inclusivity, the social activism, the acceptance of uncertainty and the absence of a single creed.

This, it seemed, was spirituality and community for people who didn't readily conform, who were prepared to question and challenge, had a social conscience and a genuine and forward thinking desire to improve society. There was no pushiness or proselytising, no grand and certain vision of God which excludes others. It seemed to fit our values and outlook. But life got in the way and we never took it further.

In any case, Quaker thought is centred on the individual's experience of God and spirituality. My impression is that 'Friends' coalesce around common values and ways of being rather than beliefs. Ask three Quakers their opinion on a spiritual matter and you will probably get nine different answers. That is, in part, its attraction but in my particular circumstances at this time it doesn't necessarily meet my need for a single coherent framework in which I can understand and accept loss and bereavement.

I set this out not to promote my own position – which is just as likely to be wrong as anybody else's – but to explain the context for my spiritual response to Louise's death. For the purposes of this book, it would be more convenient to ignore the spiritual aspect because I am painfully aware that this is not an easy subject to address and I have absolutely no desire or intention to offend, especially those members of Louise's family and friends who are dearly precious to me but who have a different perspective.

However, it would not be honest to sidestep the issue because what has happened to Louise, and what is continuing to happen to me, has prompted me to carefully examine all my rather vague and lazy assumptions and to engage at a much more personal and immediate level with the concept of an afterlife.

I attach no blame to God for what has happened. I am not angry with Him. I sometimes ask why this should have happened to us, what Louise and I have done to deserve this fate, but the questions are rhetorical. My God does not have an interventionist approach to this domain. Our lives are what we make of them. But I do ascribe to God responsibility for what happens next, the afterlife. And inevitably I spend a lot of time thinking about what is happening to Louise now, wondering whether she continues to exist in some form or other, hoping against hope that her suffering is over and she is happy, that she can continue to hear me, that she can continue to be with me, to support me in some vague and ill-defined manner which is beyond my comprehension.

But the more I think, the more I wonder again. I have to make, as my starting point, the assumption that some form of afterlife exists. Not necessarily because I am convinced of it but because the concept of nothingness not only offers no comfort but is also utterly incomprehensible. But then what form does this afterlife take? The traditional visions of angels, clouds and harps seems slightly absurd, designed perhaps to operate as a form of social control for an uneducated, downtrodden and feudal medieval society.

So what does it look, feel and smell like? What is Louise now experiencing? Since suffering is permitted in this life, why do we automatically seem to hold to the view that heaven has none, that it is a place of perfection? How can I know that Louise is happy, that her suffering is at an end, that she is fulfilled and loved, that she is reunited with her father, her grandparents and everybody else she would choose to be with? It's convenient and comforting to believe these assumptions certainly, but why should they be so?

Questions, inconsistencies and contradictions tumble out. I want to think that Louise is able to continue to enjoy in heaven everything that she took pleasure in on earth. Trees, flowers, birds, music, singing, performance and painting. I need to know that there are country lanes in which she can cycle, hills and mountains in which she can walk, seas and rivers in which she can swim, and beaches and fields in which she can walk, run and jump. I can create idyllic visions of what Louise now has.

But when I think about it logically, none of it makes sense. Louise lived in a particular place at a particular time. Why should heaven specifically replicate the nicer aspects of the British Isles and middle class British culture in the early 21st century? It might just as easily be primeval swamp, Han dynasty China, or a recreation of the conditions on some unknown planet in another corner of the universe. Can it be all of these at the same time, offering people an idealised version of the culture and geography they happened to be born into? Is it defined by the limits of our imaginations and experiences? Or is it like nothing we can imagine? If it is the latter, it may be a wonderful place but Louise will still no longer be able to enjoy all that she loved so much.

And then there are the practical aspects of the afterlife. Since a part of me, in Louise, is now there, I am desperate to understand how it works. I try so hard to maintain a conversation with Louise but it constantly flounders on not knowing her reality. When I wish her good night and sweet dreams, as I go to bed, am I wasting my breath? Does heaven have a concept of day and night? Do people need to sleep? Even if it does and they do, why should the time zones match ours? It seems to be stretching things somewhat to assume that the afterlife works on Greenwich Mean Time.

Similarly, when I ask Louise whether she has had a good day it seems rather superfluous. She is in heaven. How can she not have a good day? But then without the experience of bad days how can one truly measure and enjoy good? By the same token, work must exist for leisure time to have any meaning or value. It was one of Louise's greatest pleasures in her life. But surely, by definition, there cannot be sickness to heal in heaven so this must now be denied her.

And if Louise is as genuinely happy and healthy as I hope and assume, how can I persist in selfishly wishing for her return, to bring her back to her earthly existence? I should be grateful and happy for her that she is able to enjoy such a wondrous realm – but I'm not. I persist in wishing that she was back in this imperfect world with, by implication, the same anxieties, challenges and difficulties that she sought to escape from. What kind of love is that?

Then there is the question of how Louise relates to this world, if at all. Does she hear my prayers and those constant one-sided conversations with her? Does she see and feel my distress? If so, how could she possibly be happy knowing what I am going through? I want her to be with me as I go through my day, to be able to feel her presence as a means of comfort and support. Some people claim that they feel their loved ones with them. In truth, I don't. I feel guilty in admitting that, as though it is some form of confession that our love was not strong enough to transcend the inconvenient divide of death.

But in any case, if she is with me, how can she also be with her mother, her brother and sister, our nephews and nieces? They all want and deserve to feel something of Louise around them too. And how then can Louise actually spend time in heaven itself if we are constantly pulling her towards us? Shouldn't we leave her alone, in peace, to enjoy what we hope she has, instead of making selfish demands on her? The more that I need to believe in the concept of heaven, the more I think about it and the less likely it seems.

In my distress after Louise's death I turned, for the first time in my life, to classical Christian scripture for comfort and the answer to questions like these. Unfortunately, I didn't find the responses helpful. It was gently and lovingly explained to me that traditional thought holds that those who have died exist on a different plane, that there are not the connections I hope for. This may or may not be so. It carries a certain logic but it doesn't comfort in the way that I had anticipated.

It was a similar story in respect of my other great hope that I looked for confirmation of. That Louise and I would one day be reunited in heaven as man and wife. I had always taken my marriage vows extremely seriously. Regardless of them being within sight of God, they were vows to Louise and that was what really mattered to me. 'In sickness and in health', 'for richer for poorer'. I would honour and uphold them all. The one that I forgot about was 'till death do us part'.

It therefore came as something of a shock to learn that according to conventional Christian thought, I was no longer married to Louise, that manmade relationships were not recognised in heaven. I was initially genuinely upset by this. It seemed bizarre and contradictory that in an environment of love there is no place for the special and enduring love and commitment of two people. If true, it meant that our marriage, our relationship, really was at an end, not just comfortingly deferred to be resumed at another time and in another place. I have managed this by simply choosing to discount it. Nobody can really know if it's true. Why shouldn't I reasonably hope to be reunited again with Louise as her husband? If nothing else, it helps gets me through.

But then this comfort, in turn, leaves me with a further question that is impossible to resolve. If I am ever lucky enough to meet another woman, and feel ready to enter into another relationship, I can come to the terms with the concept that the human heart has an infinite capacity to love. I can grasp the fact that it's perfectly possible to have two wives whom you love dearly, one in this life, one not.

But what happens when we are all dead, all (hopefully) in heaven? How can I both be with Louise and my second wife simultaneously? I manage to complicate this even further by thinking about Louise's immediate needs. She did not want me to live the rest of my life alone. But she too is alone, without me, in the afterlife. If there is scope in the afterlife for love and relationships does she herself need the love of somebody else in my absence from her? However much the thought pains me, her happiness is ultimately all that matters, so if she was to find that love then she would have my blessing.

I don't understand and I am angry at the fates which mean that I have to try and think through and deal with these agonising problems. For these are no longer abstract theoretical questions for me but real and urgent. I want to resolve them in the same neat way that I can obtain definitive responses to queries on Louise's tax return or my occupational pension entitlement. But, of course, I can't.

My only option therefore, for the sake of my sanity and recovery, is to try and set my scepticism aside and allow myself to trust and believe that there are acceptable answers to all these seemingly impossible questions, but that they come in the shape of something infinitely more complex and sophisticated than either I or the accumulated wisdom of mankind is able to comprehend. I must try to trust in a universal God who will provide for Louise in her need as I would want her to be provided for, and who will allow us to – one day – be reunited in our presence and our love. I must hold on to the thought that it will all work out in the end.

Perhaps it is not for nothing that Louise's favourite psalm, and thus the only one that I know, was Psalm 46 verse 10; 'Be still and know that I am God'. I still have no certainty but my hope is more important to me than ever before.

The Little Things

It's times like tonight when I miss Louise the most. Of course I miss her all the time. I feel constantly incomplete, almost physically so, as if one of my limbs has been amputated. There is a void where she should be. But often her absence is most deeply felt at the most mundane of moments. Such as coming home from work.

It's been a tough day in the office. I ended up having to stay much later than anticipated to sort out an unexpected emergency. Tempers were fraying amongst those around me. Such is the nature of my job that much of that anger was directed towards me. None of this is new. I can deal with it. But throughout, I found myself constantly wishing with all my heart that I could tell Louise about it. That I could go home and recount the story to a sympathetic and loving audience who would be wholly on my side. Go home to a house full of light, warmth, love and human contact.

Instead, I found myself outside a darkened, eerily quiet and empty house. As usual when I am at the front door in the dark I think back to the night Louise died. I remember standing outside, trying frantically to gain entry, already knowing from the desperate note pinned to the door what I would find. When I haven't left the hall light on in readiness for my return I now always open the front door ajar, just enough to reach in, turn the light on and wait a couple of seconds, giving time for the sight of Louise as I found her to disappear, to be banished by the light.

Inside there is nobody to complain to about my day in the office, nobody to reassure me that I'm right and the rest of the world is wrong, nobody to give me a consolatory cuddle, nobody to tell me that dinner is ready, nobody to suggest that we curl up on the sofa and watch that DVD together. Nobody to share anything with. Just silence and emptiness.

Our partner is a constant presence in our life, even when they are not physically in our company. Remove that presence, that solid and reassuring ever present shape, and you have the true meaning of the void that is absence. And it tends to be the little things where the absence of our soulmate is most noticeable. It's not so much the loss of somebody to share those major life experiences with: family celebrations, changing jobs, moving house, holidays. Nor is it being deprived of the physical relationship with our sexual partner. All of this is highly significant in its own right but the very greatest impact is the loss of those daily moments of quiet intimacy, understanding, anticipation, and support which perhaps before were so routine that we took them for granted, or so intangible that we scarcely recognised their existence, let alone their value.

Loss of our partner is the knowledge that nobody needs to know when we are getting home, that nobody would even notice if we didn't come home at all. It's walking down the street without holding hands. It's having nobody to tell about that compliment we received at work or the joke we heard, or to patiently listen to our excitement at our club's expensive new Danish international striker. It's the lack of somebody to quietly warn our hosts in advance that we really hate mushrooms. It's having nobody to offer to make a cup of tea for. It's the absence of a reassuring presence next to us when we wake up after a nightmare. It's coming home on an evening and not speaking to another human until the following day. It's not being able to touch somebody lightly on the shoulder while passing each other in the kitchen. It's having nobody to tell us that they are proud of us. It's having nobody to be proud of.

Loss of our partner is not about being one when previously we were two. It's being half when we were previously one.

A Thousand Deaths

7th June | 135 days

I've decided that I need to take the sympathy cards down. They started arriving within 24 hours of Louise's death in the darkness of midwinter and were soon overflowing from the shelves on to the dining room table. Meals were eaten next to a forest of sorrowful messages and tributes, bottles of ketchup jostling for table space with 'thinking of you at this sad time' cards until space was cleared in the conservatory to absorb the excess.

Now, two seasons on in full summer, it seems to be time to pack the cards away in a memory box, if only to preserve them from damage. They will come down together with our last Valentines cards to each other. (Louise died three weeks before Valentine's Day but I found her card to me, unwritten, in her bedside drawer). It could be interpreted as a step forward. A sign, to use that ugly phrase, beloved of the non-bereaved but rarely used by those who have suffered real loss, of 'moving on'. Maybe it is. But for me it also feels like a step away, a further break in my bonds with Louise and one less sign of her presence within the house.

A wise friend warned me early on that for those left behind, death is a process and not an event. Every day since has borne out the truth of that, each one chalked off a mixed blessing. The passage of time eventually, imperceptibly, begins to dull the raw intensity of despair, bewilderment and hopelessness.

When I was sitting slumped on the floor of the ambulance, curled up in the foetal position, minutes after finding Louise's body, I found myself thinking 'I wish it was April'. I just wanted the next two months to disappear, to wish away the immediacy of the tragedy. I knew time would bring relief of a sort. And even though sometimes it's hard to realise in the frequent moments when grief bites back hard, it does. It just takes what feels like an eternity. Even though I can recall every moment of my time with Louise prior to 23rd January as if it was moments ago, the four months since have unravelled within their own completely separate dimension of time. The day of Louise's death, the funeral and all the events surrounding it feel as though they took place in another age. I relate to them as though they were experiences from decades ago, made remote and unreal, softened by the march of time.

But those passing days are less welcome for the distance they begin to put between Louise and I. The world moves on, and I reluctantly have no choice but to go with it, while Louise stays behind. It's now more than four months since I held her, kissed her, stroked her hair, heard her tell me that she loves me. That gap can only grow wider. Every day brings a further small change that moves Louise from the present into the past, that makes her death more irrevocable. Every single one brings fresh pain. Every time that I throw away even the smallest piece of evidence of Louise's existence; scrap paper with an inconsequential note on it in her handwriting, a receipt, or food that she will never eat, another small part of Louise dies and I feel it all over again.

Food has, in fact, been a particular emotional challenge. It took me until April to throw away the remains of the stockpile from what transpired to be our last Christmas together. There was little space in the freezer because it was full of plastic containers with the excess turkey and gammon, stuffing and mince pies, even some remnants of pecan pie from the American side of the family.

Eventually I was forced to clear it after an over-enthusiastic trip to Sainsbury's (I find it difficult to judge the right amounts of food to buy for one). I grabbed the food up as quickly as I could, ran to the bin and threw it in, not looking back. I didn't want a repeat of the Sunday afternoon which I spent in floods of tears because of the sight of a pile of frozen vegetable lasagnes laying in the bin. Every time that I discard Louise's food, not only do the comforting signs of her presence in the house diminish further, but I also feel as though I'm starving her. Her foothold in the freezer is now marked only by a single carton of vegetable soup, well beyond its use by date. I have no intention of moving it.

Those catalogues and advertising leaflets which keep on dropping through the letter box are no longer unwanted junk mail but welcome signs of life and normality. HMRC, the DVLA, the BMA and a host of other acronyms may all have had to be informed of Louise's death, painfully in each case, but there's no reason why I have to let clothing retailers or charities into the secret. Dr Louise Tebboth has pretty much passed away now. Nothing comes for her any longer. But Mrs Louise Marson lives almost every time that the postman visits.

I can capture memories of Louise, get photos enlarged, framed and displayed but these are second-hand memories, reminders of what once was. What really provides me with comfort, with the illusion that all is still well, are the signs of her active occupation of the house, practical evidence of her life. The little indications that she will come downstairs or walk through the front door any moment; the rucksack with her equipment for home visits to patients, her scarf and coat by the door, her purse, gloves and mobile phone in the lounge.

You can tell that Louise died in the winter by the type of clothing still out on display. I briefly – half seriously – considered swapping it all for items more appropriate for the new season, replacing, for instance, her winter bobble hat in the hallway with her summer baseball cap before I realised it was the insanity of grief. I do, of course, make progress of sorts. The occasional sudden burst of energy and determination might lead to a few clothes being put in a drawer, a rucksack being emptied. But moments like that are few and come at considerable emotional cost.

This reluctance to change anything, even the smallest thing, which distances us, creates an inertia. I now understand why the homes of so many elderly people look as though they have been in a time capsule for years. I have wanted to modernise parts of the house ever since we moved in. Redecoration of the hall might even help to smooth over the memories of finding Louise there. But I couldn't possibly change anything at the moment, to make the house less like the one Louise knew and we shared together. Those 1980's kitchen units have an indefinite reprieve.

I know that this isn't sustainable in the long term. I cannot hold back the tide of time. But I'm determined to continue the unequal fight for as long as possible. And tomorrow is the fifth anniversary of the first time that we met. Maybe it isn't the right time to take those cards down after all.

Understanding the Beginning

10th June | 138 days

Grief has an uncanny way of catching out the unwary or the overconfident. I've astonished myself at how well I've been coping in recent weeks. Of course, the underlying sadness, bewilderment and sense of loss is ever present but I've been conscious, four-and-a-half months in, of a steadying of the emotions and at least a partial re-engagement with the world. My concentration levels at work are much improved. I enjoyed an evening at the cricket with friends without feeling the need to constantly talk about Louise. Some sort of routine, empty though it may be, has begun to emerge. For the first time in 133 days I even went a whole 24 hours without crying.

But my pride in my resilience was misplaced. This week marks the fifth anniversary of Louise entering my life and it has completely floored me.

I didn't expect it to. I had negotiated Louise's birthday, the first in the spread of dates that were once joyful landmarks but will now forever be potential trip hazards, relatively well. And we never marked the week during which we moved from online contact to telephone conversation to a first date within days, with anything more than a fond passing comment. We invested significance in the anniversary of our wedding rather than that pizza near Victoria Station. I was confident that I had things under control. So I'm taken aback to find myself returned to a state of vulnerability, of raw overwhelming despair and rivers of tears.

It was probably not a good idea to look back once again at those first emails or to recall, through my diary entries, those early conversations. Moments which profoundly changed the course of my life. Louise cautiously but hopefully articulating the type of emotionally intelligent and fulfilling relationship she dreamed of. Words which now jump off the screen and bring to life once again the person that I came to know more intimately than any other, and which speak so poignantly of the hopes which she was able to realise only for such a cruelly brief period. Just as a book can't properly be understood until we have turned the last page, it is only now, when I know the end of our story, that I can place the beginning in its true context. The knowledge that the hope, excitement and ideals were destined to be transformed into loss and tragedy has turned the fairy tale into something infinitely darker.

I am bewildered by the way in which Louise could explode into my life, from nowhere, take it over, become my world… and then disappear in an instant, in the time it took me to discover her body.

But as I look for solace I understand that she hasn't disappeared. Louise will remain with me forever. Not just in my heart and memories but in the tangible legacy that she has left me; my new found self-confidence, the interests she introduced me to, her influence on my way of looking at the world, my adopted 'in law' family including six nephews and nieces, her friends that became mine. Louise brought all this to me and more. Everything that I am today, and everything that I will be in the future, is down to Louise. For so long as I live, so does a part of her.

The Post Mortem: To Know or Not to Know

13th June | 141 days

Death brings with it a succession of intensely painful ceremonies and events which have to be endured before we are finally left alone to grieve in peace; the farewell visit to the undertakers, the funeral, the memorial service (two in Louise's case), the scattering of the ashes. Now, after months of frustrating delay the very last of these hurdles is finally in sight: the inquest. This presents me with possibly the biggest and most distressing dilemma of all. How much do I want to know about the way Louise died?

Currently sitting in my email inbox, just a couple of clicks away, are copies of all the relevant papers held by the Coroner ahead of the inquest. This includes the toxicology report, the Police Statement and, most explosively, the report on the post mortem. I didn't need to have them. The official from the Coroner's Office asked if I wanted this level of disclosure. Many relatives don't and I understand why. I wish that I myself could have declined.

I found Louise. I know how she killed herself. I don't need to know the detail or extent of her suffering or the nature of the injuries sustained in the act itself. Every day since, I have tried hard – with some success – to suppress thoughts of Louise's final moments. It's been a step too far, the one thing that I cannot cope with. On occasions when I have found myself speculating, I have broken down. And looking back is becoming harder as the days go past. I used to read Louise's farewell note almost every day. Now I cannot bring myself to so much as glance at it. It's as if my brain is telling me that it's had enough. It needs some respite.

I fear the potential destructiveness of the knowledge contained in those email attachments. I need to protect myself if I am to make the recovery and lead the life that Louise would wish for me. Once I have opened the document, there can be no going back. What is read cannot be unread. The pictures that it will conjure up in my mind will remain with me for the rest of my life. It does not have to be this way. While I am obliged to attend the inquest to give evidence I have the option of leaving the courtroom at the point the post mortem is addressed. I can choose to remain in ignorance.

But the freedom to choose is an illusion. I feel compelled to know. Not for me but for Louise. It is my duty as her husband to share in what she went through.

Our marriage vows did not only apply to the good times. Just as it was right that it was me who found Louise's body and not a stranger, an unknown policeman or paramedic, I must even now be there for her as far as I humanly can. I hope that somehow, in some way, my sharing in the knowledge of what she suffered will make Louise feel less alone. It is the closest that I can get to being there with her in the moment of death.

For the same reasons I know that I will not be able to leave the courtroom to avoid hearing the evidence. To do so would feel as though I am abandoning Louise and I cannot contemplate that. I want her to know that I am with her, that she is not alone. I know that I am risking my mental wellbeing for the sake of a gesture but gestures are the only way in which I can now show Louise my love and commitment and they are therefore deeply meaningful.

I will read the report and know. I must.

Fighting Back...
Sometimes

19th June | 147 days

It's very easy, and in many senses comfortable and rewarding, to assume the role of victim that society wants to assign to me. I receive sympathy, favours, and have few expectations placed upon me. I barely need to make it out of my front door fully dressed to be praised for my strength and bravery.

This can be very gratifying and rewarding. There are times when I genuinely need those allowances and favours and that sympathy; times when I want to pour my heart out to the stranger on the other end of the phone line, or to the supermarket cashier or the hairdresser. Times when I need to tell them that my wife has died and I am broken and to receive their support and understanding – or at least soothing noises which I optimistically choose to interpret as understanding.

Occasionally – and I say this with no pride – I have even used my victimhood to manipulate situations to my advantage. It's amazing how much better service you can receive from a call centre, or how quickly you can send nuisance marketing calls packing, when you drop into the conversation the fact that your wife has recently taken her life. I possess a trump card which I can play in almost any circumstance. Get out of jail free.

But, increasingly, there are times when I want to break out of the straightjacket of mourning, when I am suffocated by the shocked or awkward response of strangers, the preferential treatment, the widened eyes, the sympathetic look and tone of voice. And perhaps most of all by the sense of obligation, to be constantly having to thank everybody for the kindness they are showing to me. When your entire self-image, and your designated role within your marriage, has been that of the 'rock', the person who provides stability, it's humiliating to suddenly be perceived as vulnerable and in need of special consideration.

In these moments, I want to be normal again, to pass incognito. I want to be given permission to leave, at least momentarily, what the author and blogger Helen Bailey describes as "Planet Grief", that strange and all-encompassing environment where bereavement becomes your only identity, your only experience, your only way of seeing and interpreting the world around you.

I have been grieving constantly for nearly five months now. Other than when I am at work, every single waking moment is spent in some form of activity related to Louise's death, be it writing my diary or this book, engaging on-line or in person with others in similar circumstances, reading about grief, loss or suicide, or archiving Louise's life and the precious records of our relationship. I have been dealing with the administrative requirements, talking to or about Louise, memorialising her in obituaries and works in her name. It's emotionally and physically exhausting.

I have become so lost in this subterranean world of darkness that I forget the one that I used to inhabit still exists. I found myself looking at photos of couples the other day and wondering which one of them was dead. It startled me to remember that neither of them were. *Newsflash! In some marriages both partners are still alive.* Worse, when I do encounter this strange normality I can react to it ungenerously, jealous of people whose partner still breathes.

I don't want to continually feel as though I am something of a freak, even though, statistically speaking, I know that I am. Approximately 1 adult male in every 350 under the age of 50 is widowed in the UK. That makes me, if not quite a freak, then at least something of an oddity. But only around 1,300 women take their lives in the UK each year, or in other words about 1 in 20,000. To be that 1 in 20,000 widower, even assuming that each of those women was married, is undoubtedly freakish.

It's a curious feeling to be such an outlier because to me I'm just… me. There is nothing abnormal about my wife taking her life at the age of 40. It's my reality, my normal. I know no different. It's people whose husbands and wives are still alive, who have managed more than three or four years of marriage, who are the oddities, not me.

When I am feeling strong, I want to resist the victimhood, the world that I find myself in, the exceptionalism. I want to metaphorically put two fingers up at my fate and proclaim that I will survive and even be stronger for the experience. Bloody-minded resistance isn't necessarily my strong point but this is the only life I have and I need to make the best of it, even if it isn't the one that I expected or had chosen for myself. Louise doesn't have a second chance. I do, and I owe it to her to approach it positively, particularly as one of the reasons she took her life was because at that moment in time, in the depths of her darkness, she thought it would free me to enjoy a better future. If I curl up into a ball and allow this to defeat me, I will have failed Louise and made her sacrifice even more pointless, even more tragic.

Of course I struggle. Lots. I'm lethargic, my sleep patterns are chaotic, I get into work late and am sometimes present in the office more in body than spirit. I'm not eating enough vegetables (Louise would be gently disapproving at the lack of colour on my plate). I haven't summoned up the strength to move or sort through, much less dispose of, Louise's possessions. I don't have the concentration span or motivation to read a book or watch a TV programme. I cheat with the housework by having somebody in, to clean once a fortnight.

But despite all this, on balance I am sometimes rather proud of myself. This is the most difficult and challenging time of my life. I have dealt with events and emotions that I never dreamed I would have to confront, that are beyond the experience, or maybe even the imagination, of most people. I found my wife dead in horrific circumstances, summoned up the strength to make the calls to inform family and friends, returned to the house within 24 hours and adapted to living here again, alone (the first time, in fact, that I have ever lived on my own).

With some assistance I arranged the funeral, visited Louise, or at least a waxy representation of her, in the funeral parlour and steeled myself to kiss that cold, lifeless and not entirely convincing likeness goodbye. I survived the trauma of the funeral, the unreality of sitting through a service staring at a coffin which contains the body of my wife. I managed to hold myself together sufficiently to deliver a coherent eulogy to her in front of hundreds of people at not one but two memorial services.

I have mechanically worked through the paperwork and bureaucracy that comes with death, every telephone call and letter of notification representing a mini death, the closure of another part of Louise's life. I have battled with the incompetency of the Coroner's Office, negotiated the Mental Health Trust's investigation and final report. And I stood in our favourite local beauty spot scattering the ashes that were once my best friend, my lover, my wife, my inspiration and my hope.

Each and every one of these events would, individually, represent the worst moment of my life. But, of course, they don't occur in isolation. One leads to another and the brutality of the collective trauma is overwhelming, exhausting, disabling. And in some senses the time in-between is even more difficult to deal with. The sheer grim and lonely reality of the day-to-day grind of life without Louise.

And yet here I am, still standing, still functioning, albeit imperfectly. And doing so without the aid of any artificial stimulants, whether alcohol or medication, or meaningful counselling. I fumble around in the darkness, trying desperately to do the right things; to help me, to help others and to honour Louise and positively represent her memory and legacy to the world. I am trying to reach out to others in support groups, resisting the temptation to withdraw into myself. I constructively process my experiences through talking and writing.

And I am working with eminent and high profile professionals in the medical world to develop a charity in Louise's honour of a scale that surprises even me, using our story as a means of assisting others.

Of course none of this is necessarily down to any particular strength of character on my part. The numbness that comes with the uncomprehending shock of bereavement, particularly sudden bereavement, has carried me a long way under its anaesthetic. On much of the journey, I have found myself simply floating downstream on the currents. I haven't made any attempt to go out and deal with events. Rather, they have come to me. All I have had to do is get through each hour and each day. In that way, time passes and things happen to me on the way.

And I haven't done anything on my own. I have had the good fortune to receive wonderful help, support and love from family and friends, to have had an understanding employer, no particular financial pressures and to have discovered the invaluable charity the Widowed and Young Foundation (WAY) which provides the lifeline that comes from contact with others in my situation, who truly understand and support each other through the mutual pain and loss. I have also had the advantage that, unlike many who lose their loved ones to suicide, I know and understand why Louise took her life. All of this has helped me through.

I often ask myself what Louise would be thinking of the way in which I am coping, and what she would be doing if the situation was reversed; if it had been me who had taken my life. Always practical and clear-minded in a crisis, she would be making a better job of things than I am no doubt. But I like to think that she would approve of most of the choices I have made on her behalf and be proud of my efforts.

Recovery is still a long way off, and it will only ever be superficial. The wounds may heal but they will always be liable to be reopened, raw and bleeding, because the scar tissue which covers them will be so thin. But I sense that I am now through the very worst. I have reached the end of the beginning. And I am still alive, still fighting, and still hoping for better. That is the biggest achievement of my life.

Putting Myself in the Dock

27th June | 155 days

Bereavement is almost always accompanied by a sense of responsibility and guilt on the part of those left behind. The relatives of people who have died of cancer agonise over whether they should have encouraged them to seek medical advice earlier or pressed for a different form of treatment; those who lost somebody in an accident find themselves wishing they had delayed them leaving the house that morning until the car with the drunken driver was safely elsewhere, or conversely, perhaps, not delayed them. The partners of heart attack victims spend the rest of their lives regretting that stressful argument they had the previous day.

But the scope for guilt seems to loom even larger where the cause of death is suicide because, superficially at least, it seems so avoidable. This was an act of Man rather than God and thus it must follow that either in some way we were responsible for it ourselves or it was within our gift to prevent it.

The sense of control over events is, to some extent, an illusion since it presumes that suicide is an act of free will determined upon while in a rational state of mind. It presupposes that the individual can clearly, logically, assess the alternatives, determine the best course of action and seek out and accept help and support at the time of crisis.

Some suicides may occur under these conditions. The person with a chronic illness who chooses to end their physical suffering, perhaps. But most do not. Instead they take place amidst a desperate all-enveloping darkness where a hunted mind fixates, perhaps for months, perhaps just for minutes, on one solution, utterly unable to see beyond it, to grasp the existence of alternatives, to understand that the outlook is not as bleak as they imagine it, or to fully recognise the impact on others of their intended course of action. There is no more genuine choice in whether to live or die here than that exercised by somebody suffering from cancer. Louise's life was at risk from her illness just as surely as if it had been a physical rather than a mental ailment.

Nevertheless there was nothing inevitable about her death. Any number of things could have prevented it, kept her safe until the crisis passed. So many, in fact, that it's almost inconceivable that it actually happened. There were countless opportunities from the point when Louise fell ill right up to her last moments of life for the safety gates to slam shut, for her to be diverted onto another, safer course.

Most of these events were beyond my control. But I was the one closest to her, I was the person who knew her best and had the most influence on her environment. It was my duty to keep her safe. I know beyond any doubt that there were many points at which different decisions or actions on my part would have kept Louise alive.

Unlike many for whom suicide is the first, as well as the last, indication of their partner's mental distress I don't have the excuse of not knowing the risks. There were plenty of warning signs. Louise was the kindest, gentlest, most intelligent, fun-loving, energetic and warm-hearted person I have ever met and she enjoyed life with a passion which put me to shame. But she also suffered from periodic and highly distressing episodes of anxiety and depression. By the time that she took her life she had been battling a particularly severe attack of depression with incredible bravery and fortitude for several months and in the midst of this period also had to contend with the suicide of her father. Little more than a week before she died she had confessed, at the last minute, to a plan to overdose.

In the circumstances, therefore, an attempt on her life shouldn't have been a surprise. I attended the psychiatric consultations alongside Louise, talked to her about her illness endlessly and was confident that I understood, like no other person, the way her mind worked. I now have to try to come to terms with the fact that despite this knowledge I still did not save her.

I was acutely aware of Louise's distress but made a series of judgement calls about her care which, in hindsight, prove to have been wrong, or at least ineffective. I was too focused on giving her agency. Louise was extremely independent and I knew that she was distressed at the thought that she was becoming dependent upon me to keep her going. I wanted her to know that she had got better herself. I thought it would make her eventual recovery more sustainable. I therefore complied, reluctantly, with Louise's request that I return to work rather than stay by her side until she was better and accepted her reassurances, when pressed, that there was no need to alert her psychiatric care team when she went downhill again in the final few days. I tried to do what Louise seemed to want me to do rather than follow my own best instincts so that she would gain strength and empowerment from managing her own recovery.

I piled well-intentioned mistake upon well-intentioned mistake. I trusted in the robustness of the daily psychiatric monitoring programme. I trusted too much in Louise's ability as a doctor to do the impossible and manage herself as a patient and objectively and rationally assess her own state of mind. I allowed myself to be lulled into a false sense of security by the fact that she had told me about her planned overdose. I thought *that* was the moment of crisis and it had been averted. Never in my worst nightmares did I contemplate Louise returning to the idea, and so soon.

I lay in bed the next evening cuddling Louise, holding her for all I was worth, trying to come to terms with the thought that if she had carried through her plan she would now be dead and wondered how she felt about still finding herself alive. Relieved? Disappointed? Numb? I decided to wait, to give Louise time to recover before properly discussing the episode with her and telling her how much I desperately needed her to live. I feared that to confront her with such an emotionally fraught conversation when she was still fragile might be counterproductive. Maybe it would have been better had I done so.

Confused by so many ups and downs over the course of the illness, I also failed to recognise the final, crucial, dip as being anything other than part of the normal daily pattern of fluctuations which had gone before it. Maybe this was partly because I was exhausted, physically and emotionally through coping over an extended period, not only with this crisis but also another in the form of the simultaneous serious illness of my Mother. I was therefore not as alert to danger as I should have been.

Had the outcome been different, all this would have been excusable. In the absence of a hospital admission, I was in the front line of Louise's care. I knew that as the person principally responsible for creating the environment around her, every word and act on my part had the potential to influence whether she lived or died.

I felt the weight of that responsibility. The mind is an infinitely complex instrument and there are no reliable manuals or pathways to surely fix it when it is broken. Even for practitioners, psychiatry is more of an art than a science. Still, I tried hard to support Louise as intelligently and intensively as I knew how. Everything that I did appeared reasonable in context and my approach of giving her responsibility was endorsed by Louise's psychiatrist when I turned to him for advice in the final days.

Even the failure to recognise the real level of risk is understandable. It's difficult to bring yourself to seriously contemplate the idea that your wife might kill herself. The concept is too enormous, too obscene, to process. I knew that Louise had attempted suicide before but that was many years prior to us meeting. It seemed ancient history and was not something that we ever dwelt on.

People try to reassure me, to tell me that I could have done no more, that Louise was happier during our time together than at any stage in her adult life, that I may, without realising it, have helped her to survive or avoid similar moments of crisis in the past. I know that Louise herself doesn't blame me. She wrote in her farewell letter that ultimately nobody can fully hold another person. I draw some comfort from this.

But however hard I tried, however well-intentioned I may have been, however tired I was, I either did not do enough or made the wrong choices when I could not afford to do so. Only the relatives of the living have the luxury of excuses. I have to deal with a sense of responsibility for what happened, the knowledge that I failed Louise in those final days.

I replay over and over again what I could and, with hindsight, should have done differently. I still torture myself endlessly and ultimately pointlessly not only about the major decisions but also the smaller omissions. Why, for example, didn't I have the presence of mind to buy Louise flowers in the last few days? Or to tell her exactly how much I loved her and needed her? It might just have lifted her mood the fraction that was necessary to get her through the immediate crisis.

I was Louise's husband. It was my responsibility to keep her safe. I was there to support her. I was her rock. No matter what I may have done before, on this occasion, when she needed me most, I failed her. I will have to live for the rest of my days with the knowledge that I might have been able to save the life of the woman I love so deeply, but didn't. I apologise to Louise every day. It is hopelessly inadequate but it is all I now have in my power to do.

A Summer Evening Elsewhere

28th June | 156 days

I have come to dread people asking me how I am. I don't know how to respond, to come even remotely close to articulating in a few passing words the confused, powerful and often contradictory emotions swirling around within me, to describe the deep lows, the occasional highs and the almost ever-present and all-encompassing dull void. If I had several hours, a good thesaurus and a skilled counsellor to help me give form to my thoughts, I might be able to come close. In the absence of such resources, I usually settle for 'as good as could reasonably be expected in the circumstances'.

And that's not far off the mark. By and large I *am* coping better than I might have feared and at least as well as most in a similar position. When I talk to widows and widowers at an earlier stage in their journey I find myself beginning to be able to offer hope based on my own experience. The rawness *does* begin to fade a little and daily life becomes that bit less unbearable. I know that I'm getting there, even if I don't know where 'there' is. The important thing is that isn't the place I have been inhabiting for the last five months. Anywhere but there.

But the shock of losing Louise in such sudden and violent circumstances is so profound, the depth of the pit of despair out of which I have to climb is so deep, and the transformation of my life, both the immediate day to day and the long term future, is so complete, that my recovery is inevitably slow and fragile. It follows a path which is littered with obstacles, road blocks and diversions. I hit one of those obstacles today.

Visiting the local beauty spot where Louise's ashes are scattered is always emotional. But this evening, with the warm sun on my back, I was carried away to other beautiful summer evenings in much happier circumstances: the numerous times we strolled together amidst the trendy metropolitan crowds on Louise's beloved South Bank, the long mid-summer daylight hours enjoyed on the implausibly beautiful white beaches of Mull, watching the breathtaking sunsets of the Peloponnese, cycling the country lanes of Suffolk, listening to the hauntingly beautiful wail of the call to prayer echoing across ancient Istanbul, wandering in the hopelessly romantic, tangled and faded backstreets of old town Ragusa. To countless warm, peaceful evenings when we cuddled, held hands, kissed, loved and lived.

I yearned to be back there. Safely in Mull in 2012, the Peloponnese in 2013, Sicily in 2014. In a time when we were together, life was good and the future certain. I wanted, in fact, to be anywhere but here, in Surrey in 2015, lonely and lost.

As the sun set, barely 50 yards away a bride and groom were posing for a photographer who was attempting some of those almost obligatory ethereal shots of couples in bucolic surroundings and dreamy contemplation of everlasting love and devotion. Four years ago, that was Louise and me, dazed and excited, taking directions from our wedding photographer. Now I was sitting on a bench telling a tree about my week. I wanted to shout out to the couple, to warn them not to take the future for granted, to grab and savour every precious moment, to appreciate it and live it as if it were their last together. Because one day, if not sooner than later, it will be.

Shifting Realities

5th July | 163 days

Louise took her life five months ago. I know this because the calendar tells me so but such has been the distortion in my subsequent perception of time and reality that it might just as easily have been five days ago, or even five years. I have become completely disconnected with the passage of time and confused about my relationship to the world around me – what is real and what is not.

The day that Louise died sits on a fault line. There is before and there is after and the way in which I sense and experience time and events is starkly different either side of that fissure. On one side sits reality and on the other something much less clearly defined. The problem comes in telling which is which.

Until very recently, the real world was, emphatically, the one which Louise and I shared. It may have been months since I last saw her but our time together and her presence was so tangible that I felt I could reach out and touch her. It seemed as though it was only moments previously that we were cuddled up together on the sofa watching a DVD, walking down the road hand-in-hand or exploring the Sicilian countryside on our last holiday. I could feel her, smell her, hear her voice. I could very easily imagine her walking through the door or coming down the stairs at any moment. Louise may have been dead but her life and our relationship was still real and solid. It had presence and immediacy.

Conversely, the events since Louise's death felt as though they had unravelled in slow motion over an impossibly long time. Nothing that had happened in that period seemed remotely real, from the stunning shock of the night of the 23rd January through Louise's funeral and beyond into the small landmarks and 'firsts' of day-to-day life without her. I could remember the events, I had witnessed them but I barely felt them. It was as if I was watching a film portraying somebody else's life in 3D. It was immersive but somehow not quite real. Certainly not *my* personal experience. I couldn't relate to it or own it.

Even the simple words 'Louise's death' baffled me. I rolled them round in my head and on my tongue, trying hard but failing to understand how Louise could be associated with a state which applied to… well, the dead. Death was something which happened to the elderly, and people on TV – usually in a far distant country. If it touched *people like us* then it was restricted to those unlucky enough to be struck down with serious physical illness or affected by tragedy. Louise was young, physically healthy and, being my wife, clearly exempted from any form of tragedy. To apply the language of death, words like 'funeral', 'cremation', 'ashes', 'memorial', 'post mortem' or 'inquest' to her made no more sense than it would if two different languages were used in the same sentence. I understood the meaning of both but couldn't work out how the words could possibly belong together.

But now things are even more muddled. There has been a partial reversal of my perception of reality in recent weeks. Sometimes I find myself accepting that the real world is the one that is all around me. It's now. It's widowhood, loneliness and a constant internal hum of sadness, sometimes louder, sometimes quieter but always present: the tinnitus of grief. Above all, it's the fact of Louise's death and our enforced separation.

I still don't understand what has happened and find myself bewildered by it. No doubt this confusion isn't helped by the jangling juxtaposition of conflicting realities all around me.

On the one hand, the void created by Louise's physical absence speaks of loss and change. On the other, Louise's possessions remain in place. Her clothes are hanging up in the wardrobes, her books are on the bookshelf, her lotions and potions are in the bathroom, her medication is in the medicine cabinet. Her rucksack for home visits to patients is packed, her notes and reminders are on the fridge door. If she were to return now all she would need to bring with her would be a new toothbrush. Everything else is ready for her to pick up again. I am trying to understand what the finality of death means while being surrounded with the material evidence of life, a life merely paused and ready to be resumed at a moment's notice.

But I am steadily beginning to acknowledge the new reality. Less and less do I find myself shaking my head in disbelief and thinking 'this can't be happening to me'. It now, sometimes, feels more relevant and more accurate to describe myself as a widower than it does to say that I am married – even if the concept, the real meaning behind the term 'widower', remains far too large for me to grasp when I apply it to myself.

This may be a healthy sign of acceptance and normalisation. However, at the same time as my focus is adjusted to bring the present into sharper definition, what went before is becoming distressingly blurred and indistinct. On occasion, it's now difficult to believe that I was once married, that I shared my life with Louise. It feels fantastical, almost as if it were a figment of my imagination. I now need to listen to recordings to recall Louise's voice. The sight of her in a photo brings me up short, a sudden shock that reminds me of what really was. I look at my wedding ring and almost wonder how it got on my finger.

The best four-and-a-half years of my life have been snatched away from me and converted into an increasingly distant memory, little more real to me now than the early years of my childhood. I have to stretch further and further if I still want to reach out and touch it. I am losing Louise and I am losing my sense of myself during our time together. My reality is shifting into the painful present but in doing so it is denying me my cherished past.

The Grace of Grief

11th July | 169 days

One wouldn't expect to find any beauty in grief. It can appear an unrelentingly dark place; the loneliness and isolation, the shock, the sadness, the despair, the anger, the guilt, the fear, the exhaustion, the hysteria, the uncertainty and insecurity, the lethargy, the restlessness, the jealousy, the bewilderment. It's numbing and soul destroying. Never have I felt more dead. And yet paradoxically rarely have I felt more alive.

When it is not dulled and anaesthetised by numbness, grief brings with it a startling intensity of emotion. We are stripped raw, reduced to a childlike state of vulnerability and need. Unable any longer to process thought as the rational adult we are accustomed to believing ourselves to be, we instinctively fall back on a much more primitive response to the position we find ourselves in. We feel rather than think.

And while much of what we feel is desperate, dark and destructive, this heightened level of stimulation also allows us access to a range of positive emotional responses and a relationship with the world around us which is more powerful and pure than anything I have previously encountered. While I have lost my ability to connect with, or care about, much which I previously thought to be important, the trivialities, preoccupations and stresses of day-to-day life, I find myself blessed with an enhanced awareness of genuine and meaningful beauty, a stronger empathy for others, a more acute appreciation of the value of life and, above all, a depth of love for Louise which for all the pain it now brings is a privilege to experience.

Grief is not only the price of love. It is its ultimate manifestation. I have noted before that Louise's death has seen me fall in love with her all over again. Or rather, since we never fell out of love in the first place, it has taken what already existed, what I already thought was special, to new levels of intensity.

It's only now that I can fully appreciate, through its absence, exactly how much Louise gave to me, what her presence meant to me and the difference she made to the world around us. This realisation, coupled with the heart-rending knowledge that it is all lost, has nurtured a love of startling purity. Of such purity, in fact, that it can almost only exist within the space which bereavement creates. For all Louise's remarkable inner beauty, it would be impossible to sustain for any length of time should it be actually tested by the reality and familiarity of her living presence. And while the depth of the love is true and enduring, its urgency is simply exhausting.

Of course the strength of this emotion makes the hurt and loss even more painful to endure, but now that I am a little way into this journey I can see that it also provides comfort and a sense of pride and gratitude to have the opportunity to feel so deeply for somebody so special.

This new understanding of the potential of love extends beyond Louise. I find my capacity to appreciate and celebrate the very existence of love, the gift it gives to others, has also been greatly enhanced. Not, it must be said, that this is easy when I am confronted by couples enjoying what I once had. But beneath the jealousy, the desire to run away as fast as possible to protect myself from more hurt, I can still find myself celebrating the perfect beauty of the love they enjoy in a way that I wouldn't have done prior to Louise's death.

This is all the more the case when I read tales of new love shared by the extraordinarily resilient and compassionate on-line community of widows and widowers to which I now belong. My biggest breakdown in recent days came when I was touched to the core by the moving symbolism of a photo shared within that same community which showed the new bride of a widower laying flowers on the grave of his late wife on their wedding day.

I have also discovered that having been in the darkest of places myself, my capacity to identify with and understand the suffering of others has been enhanced. I know what it is like to experience the worst life can throw at you and I find my heart going out more and more frequently to those who are vulnerable and in need of support. It would be a fitting legacy for Louise if I subsequently prove strong enough to be able to harness this compassion and empathy into constructive action, even as the rawness of loss and grief fades.

And if the emotion engendered by grief can heighten our appreciation of the beauty of people and relationships, the experience can do the same for the way we relate to life. Now that the fragility and transience of existence has been crushingly brought home to me I have a more urgent need to live life now, not to wait, because nobody can know what tomorrow might bring. I am impatient to feel sufficiently rested and emotionally strong enough to begin to re-engage with the job of living.

Part of this sense of life is a newfound awareness and appreciation of nature, of the simple beauty which Louise can no longer enjoy. I now understand its true meaning and worth. I realise that it is a privilege and not an automatic right to be in a position to experience such things and must not squander the opportunity that I have to do so. For the first time in my life, I find myself stopping to admire flowers, listen to the birds singing, touch the bark of a tree for the sheer sensory pleasure. These are things that Louise found joy in and in my desire to see the world through her eyes I find that I have the capacity to appreciate what I previously couldn't. I only wish that I had benefited from this wisdom and insight during her life so that I could have joined her in this appreciation more fully.

It is, of course, wrong to romanticise. There is no nobility in widowhood or grief. It is not a state that anybody would choose and in many respects it can make us very unattractive: withdrawn, pre-occupied, angry and jealous. But in her perpetual search for spiritual enlightenment, Louise used to talk about the power and gift of grace. I always struggled to understand the concept, unable to pin down this mysterious state. But since she died I have come to appreciate that with her generosity, wisdom, selflessness, bravery and compassion, Louise was the epitome of grace and I like to think that in some small way the heightened sense of love, empathy and appreciation of beauty which I now experience is her gift of grace to me.

Curator of the Archive

18th July | 176 days

Louise was the least materialistic person that I've ever known. She wasn't particularly interested in jewellery, had a relatively modest wardrobe, and was content with the most basic of electrical goods. If she treated herself, it was much more likely to be on an experience, a holiday, meal or trip to the theatre, than the purchase of any kind of possession. And yet over 40 years she still accumulated a household's worth of articles, each of which have their own story to tell, their own place in Louise's life and a sentimental value attached to them that has been transformed since 23rd January.

I suddenly find myself the keeper of all Louise's goods. I am bewildered by the way in which items which Louise possessed when we met have now become solely mine. Most of the contents of the house fall into this category as I brought little of my own into our shared life. From the bed to the sofa right down to simple kitchen utensils and crockery, everything speaks to me utterly of Louise and now seems out of place, as if it should have ceased to exist at the same time as she did. Surely, if I am preparing dinner using Louise's chopping board, knives and oven gloves, she must be on her way home from work to share it with me? How can they possibly have an existence independent of her?

Over time, these unremarkable and practical items will break or wear out and even I will have to bow to the inevitable and accept the need to replace them, difficult though it will be. Of even more profound emotional significance, however, are the personal effects which fill boxes, draws, shelving and loft space: photo albums, exam certificates, girlhood scrapbooks and school reports, notebooks, drawings and paintings, books, CDs, pottery, holiday souvenirs, Louise's rather random nature collection – pine cones, conkers, dried leaves. These sacred relics are a true archive of Louise's life, a reflection of her soul and spirit.

But what am I to do with it all now? I know that if the situation was reversed, Louise would have disposed of most of my possessions by this stage. But unlike her, I'm a sentimentalist and hoarder even at the best of times. Now, at the worst of times, I am paralysed by the depth of meaning contained within this archive. I am solely responsible for its safekeeping and feel the weight of that task.

In many cases, I don't know what was emotionally significant for Louise and what wasn't, and therefore can't risk discarding anything. For four-and-a-half years I slept with her in a bed covered with a well-worn woollen orange and green blanket. She never spoke about its heritage. It was only when I decided I needed to wash it and saw its label that I suddenly realised this was the very same blanket brought back from her gap year in Kenya at the age of 18 and fondly recalled by her university contemporaries at her memorial service. Petrified of damaging such a precious object, something which accompanied Louise throughout her entire adult life, I still haven't got round to washing it.

As if by some magical process of osmosis, the significance of items like this has transferred to me. Somehow, Louise's life seems to have taken over my own. They mean more to me than my own possessions. They almost certainly mean more to me than they did to Louise. In the event of a fire or other catastrophe they would be the items that I would scramble to save first.

Nevertheless, there is something slightly absurd about the consequences of this sentimentality. Am I to keep books I will never read, CDs I will never listen to, photos of people I never met, and places I never visited simply because they were Louise's? Combined with my own items it means that I travel heavy. One person with the possessions of a couple. It will take a special woman to accept me bringing Louise's physical as well as emotional legacy into a new relationship. I should attempt some sort of rationalisation. Even if I may not be able to discard Louise's dresses, surely I can get rid of her socks? I expect I shall eventually but the emotional energy it would consume is far beyond me at present.

Holding on to Louise's possessions outside the context of her life can sometimes jar. She kept a photo of me by her side of the bed. It was taken when I proposed to her in several feet of snow in Berlin's Tiergarten. When she was alive, its display was a sweet gesture of love. Now, when I am the sole occupant of the bedroom, it looks curiously narcissistic.

These are problems faced by generations of widow(er)s. But modern life presents an extra layer of challenge, one so new that customs and norms have barely been established; what to do with the digital legacy of your loved one?

Again, Louise's footprint was relatively light and yet still there are responsibilities and quandaries. What do I do with her Facebook page and email account? Louise wasn't a heavy user of Facebook but there will be private messages with friends, shared photos and status updates. Throwaway ephemera turned into precious fragments of life. I don't know Louise's Facebook login details and therefore daren't open the app in my profile on my tablet because it's the only place where it defaults to Louise's account and gives me access to these things.

Even more significantly, Louise's email account contains thousands of conversations over most of her adult life. In the modern day absence of letters, it's the single largest resource of Louise's words, moods and thoughts and the most accurate record of her activity.

I have agonised before about the morality and wisdom of accessing any of the Facebook messages or emails. Those that I have not already seen were not intended for me and I am uneasy about reading them. I know that sometimes I might not like what I find, things which were written in the pain of Louise's anxiety. In any case, death does not end the right to privacy. But I need to hold open the possibility that I might find some comfort and understanding in being able to read some of these communications one day. I cannot bring myself to close the accounts. It's too painfully final. What if Louise one day needs to send an email from heaven?

It's not just Facebook. Louise keeps popping up everywhere I go online using our shared devices. Ironically I even had to log out of her Guardian user profile before commenting in my own right on a recent article on this very subject of digital legacies. When I mentioned this, one well-meaning respondent explained how to clear the cookie settings to prevent it happening again. It rather missed the point. I *want* to be enveloped in Louise's online persona, not to delete it.

Possibly the most precious record of our relationship is our text conversations. Far more than email, the exchanges provide a real flavour of our lives together and the way we interacted; how we joked, sympathised and declared our love for each other. With the assistance of recovery software I have managed to piece together the majority of our texts to each other over the last two years, painstakingly saved the files and printed off 600 pages in hard copy form, including the last communication that we ever had, our texts in the hours prior to Louise's death. Reading these exchanges is the closest I can get to re-living a conversation with Louise. I am grateful I had the foresight to preserve them. Shortly afterwards most of the records on my mobile phone were inadvertently wiped. For a few heartbreaking hours my phone sat in the state it was in last November, the 'most recent' text at the top of the list, from Louise, simply reading 'I'm so much looking forward to giving you a big cuddle when you get in xxxxxxxxxx'.

My phone, in fact, has been slower even than me to recognise the new reality. Since I can't bring myself to delete Louise from my contacts, and my sister shares the same name, it is constantly trying to ring her. Every time I give a voice command to call my sister it asks 'Do you mean Louise (wife) or Louise (sister)?'

As the text printouts suggest, I have become obsessed with collating and backing up every digital record of Louise's existence which I can find; photos, videos, documents. I am consumed with the risk of loss, of the fragility of the digital file, of obsolescence, incompatibility, theft, accidental deletion, file corruption.

We record and store more than any generation before us but may pass down less than any since the early days of writing. I fear fires that damage hard copies, burglaries that remove storage devices, solar flares that wipe hard drives. I am only satisfied if I have all bases covered: electronic, hard copy and remote access copies of everything. One evening last week I was horrified to realise that our official wedding photos hadn't been backed up to the cloud. I couldn't leave it until the following day in case the house burnt down overnight. I sat up until 4am tagging and uploading them.

What I will eventually do with this enormous archive is open to question. It's likely that I will only ever look at a fraction of it and there are no children to pass it on to. It will die with me. But for the moment there is comfort in knowing that it will be there, as if somehow it enables part of Louise still to exist, her voice still to speak.

It's a heavy responsibility to archive and preserve a life. Not only do I now live life for both of us, I maintain Louise's past for her too.

Hope and Confusion

24th July | 182 days

Anniversaries take on a particular emotional significance for the newly bereaved, even half anniversaries. Six months ago, yesterday, Louise took her life. In the process, the life that I was living, and thought that I was going to live, was violently wrenched away from me. In the time it took me to read the note left on the front door I was transformed from a contented, proud and fulfilled husband to a lonely and despairing widower.

In the days and weeks that followed, I could really only understand two things; Louise was gone and I was broken. When I tried to peer into my future I saw nothing. Almost a complete void. All my life, every aspect of it, had been uprooted. I had no idea where I would live, when, or indeed whether, I would be able to return to work, how I would spend my time and who I would spend it with.

The only thing that *was* clear was that the coming months would bring nothing but the greatest darkness and pain of my life. I knew that it was impossible to avoid the despair and sadness that grief brings. However overused it may be, the journey as metaphor is appropriate here since grief is a state of moving from one emotional place to another. You can't go round it, over it or under it and you certainly can't turn round and go back. The only option is to put your head down, accept and absorb everything that is thrown at you and to walk through the desert until conditions slowly improve and eventually you reach the other side. I had no map for that journey and no idea how long it was likely to take. It was one I had to make alone. My life would be on hold for its duration.

Six months on, I have no clearer idea of where that journey will take me, what my 'new normal' will look like. I have, of course, established routines, coping mechanisms and rituals designed to get me through each day and deal with the loss and sadness. But they are temporary measures rather than a long-term settlement. Almost everything remains unknown and in flux.

I am still in shock. Six months is not sufficient time to recover from the impact of the loss of the focus of your love, pride, hope and future, let alone the sight of Louise in such violent and dreadful circumstances and the knowledge of both her mental and physical pain and suffering. Life has an unreal air to it. I have moved through the past six months in the same way as I relate to a dream, experiencing but not totally feeling or understanding a world that is something like the one I recognise but bizarrely and disturbingly different in so many crucial ways.

I still live every aspect of my life in the shadow of the deepest sadness. Once I shut the front door behind me when I come home from work I am hit by a deafening crescendo of silence and an emptiness which never fails to cut me to the quick. The slightest trigger – a photo, the sight of Louise's handwriting, an old email, anything which shows her as a whole person, alive with the joys and possibilities of life – is still guaranteed to reduce me to tears.

I still cry on most days though it is no longer remarkable when I do not. I go to bed in the middle of the night, not because I can't sleep but because my brain is too active to allow me to stop thinking and because my body is too tired to make the effort to move from the sofa. And there is, in any case, no longer anything for me in bed – no companionship, no love, no security, no intimacy, no sex. Just a blank.

Nevertheless, I have an admission to make. I hesitate to do so because of the guilt it brings and my fear of misinterpretation. In some senses it is the hardest thing I have had to say along this journey because it does not conform to expectations…

I am essentially doing okay. Better than I had anticipated, better than I had dared to hope. I am beginning, if not to live again, then at least to think about how I might soon do so. I am beginning to contemplate making plans for my future. I am proud of myself for dealing with, and overcoming, some of the worst possible circumstances that life could throw at me.

If I had been told as I sat in the foetal position on the floor of the ambulance on that cold and dark January evening that my life could go on, that it still held something for me, I wouldn't have believed it. And yet I am beginning to sense something strange. Something completely absent for so long. Not perhaps 'hope' as such but at least the anticipation of it. The glimmer of light that I first discerned a month ago is continuing to grow.

Something is changing. Perhaps it's acceptance and an understanding that this is now my life. Not the one that I wanted or planned but the only one that I have. I am less emotional and more composed. When I cry, the character and intensity of the act has changed. I no longer find myself shaken by volcanic eruptions of tears of an intensity and physicality far beyond anything which I have ever known or suspected might be possible. I no longer find myself lying on the floor literally writhing in the agony of the emotional pain. My tears are real and sad but more conventional in their flow and volume. They are tears recognisable to the non-bereaved.

I am learning how to manage the loneliness. I am beginning to become accustomed to visiting friends on my own. That space on the sofa or at the dining room table next to me, where Louise should be, still gapes but I can mostly put it to the back of my mind. I have always been able to enjoy my own company and that now equips me to more easily cope with the long hours at home on my own. I have learnt to get through each evening by imagining it to simply be one night on my own, as if Louise was out, rather than merely one of an endless succession of lonely nights all following the same predictable pattern. The same as last night and tomorrow night and the night after.

While everything always comes back to Louise, I find that the periods for which I can be distracted and throw off that heavy burden of grief are becoming more frequent and of a longer duration. I am currently on my first holiday without Louise – one spent surrounded by much of her extended family – and I feel surprisingly comfortable, relieved to be free from the associations and memories of the house, and able, largely, to distract myself.

And I am beginning to look forward to certain things. To the new football season. To opening a book about something other than bereavement or spirituality for the first time since January. To a major holiday planned for the New Year. Most of all, to starting the task of building my new life. I am not ready to commence that new life yet, nor even to actively plan for it, but I now know that the day *will* come when I am ready to do so and perhaps relatively soon.

The prospect of one day opening my heart to another woman no longer seems as impossible, or as repugnant as it once did. I tease myself with visions of a future relationship that gives me back some of what I have lost, perhaps even provides something new, and allows me to openly hold and honour my love for Louise. Life is desperately, sometimes cruelly, short and I am impatient to be able to break free from this grief and live it as Louise intended me to as quickly as possible.

It's true that the shock and bewilderment, the inability to appreciate the enormity of what has happened, remain ever present. But I am coming to the conclusion that perhaps they always will. Perhaps they are beyond absorption.

All of this confuses me. Instinctively, it does not feel right. I feel guilty that I am grieving in the 'wrong' way. I worry that it means I might not have loved Louise as much as I thought and that she will be upset at the speed of my recovery. I even wonder and worry if I am capable of the kind of love that provokes extended mourning.

But I know that none of this is the case. I have already written about the depth and purity of my love for Louise. If I had it in my power to save her at the expense of my own life, to swap places, I would do so. So why, then, am I not still mired in acute distress? How can the intensity and rawness of the pain have been dulled to something which is usually much more manageable? How is it that I can now tentatively look forward as well as reflecting back?

The answer, I think, is simply the astonishing human capacity for resilience. George Bonanno, writing in *The Other Side of Sadness*, emphasises that this has been greatly underestimated. While a minority experience chronic grief reactions and risk getting stuck at that point, most people, however shocked and wounded they may be, manage to regain their equilibrium relatively quickly, at least to the point where they can start to pick up their lives again. The extent to which those people did, or did not, love is immaterial. It appears that I am not so unusual after all.

I do not want to mislead, to minimise the stunning impact of the loss of a partner at a young age. The re-emergence of hope and a sense of possibility is fragile and the concept of 'recovery' relative. The fact that, even during the course of the two days, I have been mulling over this post and have found myself broken down in tears twice illustrates that I have not yet found my way out of the desert.

In fact, in many respects, the journey has barely started. I shall have to live the rest of my life without Louise and the sadness and loss will always now be a part of me, branded on my heart. There will be plenty of difficult times to come and it is inevitable that on occasions I will stumble and retreat back into darkness. It's possible one of those stumbles could lead to a major fall. The next six months will bring the challenges of our wedding anniversary, Christmas, and the anniversary of Louise's death and the events leading up to it. I am dreading all of these for the emotional grip that they will exert, but none as much as the last public ordeal still to be endured: the inquest.

My journey therefore continues. The ground is still rough and the landscape barren. However, I now at least feel as though I have an outline of a route and can see that I am travelling in the right direction and at a quicker rate than I thought likely. I am doing okay.

The Empty House

31st July | 189 days

I wanted to provide a sense of what it feels like when you have lost your partner. When you come home and close the door behind you on an evening and find yourself alone in a silent house that was once a place of warmth, light and love. When you know that you won't speak to anybody else until the following day.

Married – Just

1st August | 190 days

I had to complete a staff survey at work this week. There were the usual questions on satisfaction with pay and rewards and understanding of corporate priorities, but as I came to the personal section my heart sank. I knew what was coming next.

I used to fret about the age category I fell into, helplessly observing my relentless march towards middle age. But now I dread responding to the inevitable questions on marital status. Sure enough here it was: Married or Single? A brutal binary choice. Black or white. But I no longer live in a binary world and the only colour I see is grey. Nothing is simple any longer, not even whether I am married.

I am one of those people, perhaps unusual amongst men, who was born to be married. I always knew that I would only find my ultimate fulfilment within an established and stable long-term relationship. I was confident that I would be a good husband. But ironically my problem was that the worthy but dull qualities which made me so suitable for that role, those of steadiness, loyalty, unselfishness and compassion, were not necessarily the type that attracts a partner in the first instance. As a consequence, what seemed to come so easily to others took me much longer to find. I searched for that special woman for 25 years, putting aside my innate shyness to suffer the indignities, insults and rejections of serial internet dating.

And then along came Louise. I could never quite believe my good fortune to have met somebody who gave me absolutely everything that I was looking for and a lot more that I hadn't dared dream of besides. While we certainly faced challenges together during Louise's periodic episodes of depression and anxiety, ours was an unusually happy, giving and gentle relationship. Not once in our four-and-a-half years together did we have an argument and the only occasion on which voices were raised was when, very near the end, she suggested that I might be better off if she were dead.

We had built an enduring relationship, one which matured beyond the unsustainable excitement of the early days to reach a point of genuine and deep understanding of each other, one in which we were able to anticipate each other's needs, accept and embrace each other's foibles, love unconditionally. It took time and hard work but we were a proper grown up couple, individuals still to be sure but part also of a new joint living organism – 'Us' – in which we were inextricably interlinked at every level.

But no sooner had I managed to clamber to the top of the mountain than I found myself swept back to the bottom again, barely having had time to pause to enjoy the view. When Louise died, so too did 'Us'. I mourn for this as I do for her. I am categorised as 'single' once more. That is undeniably how both the law and society now sees me. I am free of all marital obligations. There would be no legal impediment to me marrying again tomorrow. I am tied to nobody but this is not freedom. It means nobody knows me intimately.

I find this sudden and involuntary adjustment to my status difficult to absorb. It cuts me to the core to have to identify myself as single because I don't relate to that identity. To do so seems like a rejection of Louise. It also makes me feel something of a failure. Alone… at 46. In any case, Louise and I never fell out of love, never wanted to part. There was no decree absolute, no rejection or dissolution of our union. She remains, in my heart, mind and memory, my wife. 'Till death us do part' is the only marriage vow that I wilfully ignore.

I still think of myself as being one half of a couple. I continue to use the plural pronouns 'we' and 'our'. This is sometimes unconscious but generally I do so deliberately, despite the odd looks it provokes. It would be unthinkable to refer to 'my house' or 'my bedroom', as if I was shutting Louise out of my life, denying her continuing presence. It's unnatural not to text home to inform Louise that I'm delayed or working late. I am surprised whenever I find myself thinking about an invitation or a minor change to the house and realise that I must make the decision myself without the need to confer with her. Above all, I feel guilty whenever I think about a possible future with another woman, as if I am committing an infidelity.

My wedding ring was always symbolically important to me from the outset of our marriage. I wanted to shout from the rooftops to tell the world that I belonged to Louise. Now its significance is redoubled as proof of the continuation of the emotional ties. I continue to wear it, with immense pride. Louise's own wedding band sits next to it, on my only finger small enough to fit it. In this way we are together always. Even when I cut my finger recently I couldn't bring myself to take off my ring for just a few seconds to clean the wound. The symbolism of its removal would have been too painful. If I am ever lucky enough to one day find love again, both rings will simply transfer to my right hand. I will never hide the fact of our marriage or love.

The photos of our wedding day perform a similar function, precious proof that our four-and-a-half years together were not simply a figment of my imagination. One of the small details of Louise's end that I struggle with is the fact that, in a grotesque juxtaposition of memories and events, she died against a backdrop of our wedding photos: pictures capturing the happiest moments of our lives.

I go out of my way to avoid having to face the question of my marital status wherever I can. I dread innocent casual enquiries from strangers about my domestic circumstances because I have no ready answer to the simple question: 'are you married?' Changing the details of my next of kin on my employers HR system was one of the more emotionally challenging of the multitude of painful bureaucratic tasks that follow in the wake of death. The amendment was just a few key strokes – my sister shares the same name as Louise – but it signified a brutal transformation of my universe.

In the early days, I agonised about how I would refer to Louise in conversation. Clearly the formula 'ex-wife' would be entirely inappropriate with its connotation of divorce – little upsets the widow(er) more than its clumsy usage. So I have to settle for 'late wife' but even this implies something that is in the past whereas our marriage is still alive in everything but the strictly legalistic sense and the inconvenient absence of Louise's physical presence. Whether we call it marriage or not, I am still yours Louise, and you are still mine.

Describing the Indescribable

2nd August | 191 days

My blog now amounts to thousands of words on grief and loss. I am honoured and humbled when people thank me for articulating their own emotions. But I feel a fraud for purporting to be able to write on the subject. The truth is that no words can adequately explain the agony and despair of the death of your partner, and particularly when that death comes at such a young age, so suddenly, and so violently.

Neither my imagination nor my vocabulary is capable of conveying what it feels like to be left behind in this way; the loneliness, the confusion, the exhaustion, the shock, the guilt and the all-consuming sadness which comes to form such an established part of your daily life that you begin to forget there was a time without it.

I cannot come close to describing what it feels like to experience the complete and instant loss of love, hope, happiness and purpose from your life. I cannot begin to explain what it is like to know how much the person closest to you in life hurt and suffered, how much you hurt and suffer on their behalf. It is impossible for me to tell you what it feels like, what it truly feels like, to realise that everything which you loved about your partner and your relationship – the way you interacted, the way you spent your time together – is gone forever and can never be recaptured or recreated.

Nothing can properly describe the experience of lying on the floor convulsed in tears, crying with the whole of your body, waiting only for sheer exhaustion to bring respite and relief. I do not know how to share with you the feeling when you wake from a nightmare at 4am and instead of the reassuring and warm presence of your wife next to you there is just a void and the realisation that the nightmare is reality.

And certainly nothing can express the sense of waste which accompanies suicide, the bewilderment at the needless and senseless loss of a precious, gifted and beautiful life. The bewilderment too at the way somebody who loved life so intensely could, in the midst of a temporary darkness, deny themselves of it and in doing so deny you of them and extinguish the spark which lit your own life. Nobody can describe what it feels like to be driven to stand, in despair, cuddling the bannisters on which you last saw your wife in an attempt to reach out and try to metaphorically comfort and love her.

If you are a widow(er) yourself, then you know all or most of this. You feel it deeply, viscerally. Our journeys through bereavement may all take slightly different paths but the basic human response is universal.

If you are fortunate enough not to be in that position then I am not capable of describing the experience to you. I have to use words because I have nothing else but they do not begin to tell you what it is like to walk in my shoes. You see me when I am strong, or appear to be strong. When it is easier for me to be distracted while I am at work or amongst friends. You see me when I am struggling with all my might to be normal, or at least to seem normal. You see me on the days when I allow myself to be seen.

I wish that I could explain how it is when you do not see me. When I come home from work, or the last dinner party guests leave and I close the door behind me and am left alone. When I remove the mask that I wear in public, the one which tries to reassure everybody that I am coping. When the effort of being strong, maintaining a degree of hope and optimism, pretending to take an interest in other people's lives, becomes too much for me and I crumple, exhausted and completely hollowed out. I wish you could hear my silent scream at the disbelief and unfairness that this should happen to my amazing and wonderful, life-affirming wife - and to me. I wish that there was something you, or anybody else, could do to take the hurt away, to return me to my old life.

Grief is tidal. It comes in and it goes out like the sea. Today the waters came in and brought with them the full force of a shrieking, raging, merciless storm, one from which it is useless to even attempt to seek shelter. Today I broke down again. And while words may be inadequate to convey how it feels to grieve for Louise, to miss her from my life, I reached for them here to calm myself and to process and order my thoughts. I remain locked within a world which is beyond description but I still hope and believe in a future where the waters are calmer.

A Measure of Progress

9th August | 198 days

At just before 5pm yesterday I could have been seen jumping about in uncoordinated fashion rather like an overexcited toddler, arms flailing wildly, my face creased in an enormous smile, and at the same time heard shouting incoherently, not in despair but delight. As life events go, Brentford's injury time equaliser against Ipswich Town is as insignificant as it gets, but my response to it carries real meaning and hope.

The opening day of the football season is an eagerly awaited landmark for all supporters. This was meant to be the year that we bought Louise a season ticket so that she could more regularly and conveniently join me at matches, something she wanted to do out of love for me rather than commitment to the beautiful game. The postman recently delivered a plaintive letter from the club asking whether she would consider renewing her annual membership. Even this day on the calendar, not one of the obvious milestones or anniversaries that are so emotionally charged in widowhood, carried unavoidable memories, associations and a profound sense of loss and sadness.

But as the day wore on and I eased myself back into my matchday rituals it gradually occurred to me that the way I went about them demonstrated a measurable degree of progress in my healing in the three months since the end of last season and my previous visit to Griffin Park.

It wasn't just that I was more engaged, much more engaged, with the match in front of me, that the outcome mattered, as evidenced by the late celebrations. It was also the fact that I stopped only once or twice to miss Louise's texts enquiring after the score, that I walked with a lighter step to and from the car, and once there didn't feel the need to burst into tears that had been bottled up for several hours. It was even the fact that I drove to the game listening to Blondie. Not perhaps cutting-edge contemporary music but significantly higher tempo than the subdued tracks I have played on an almost constant loop for many months; I had given myself permission to let some noise and life into my world again.

The same sense of some form of normalisation was also apparent during dinner with wonderfully supportive friends the previous evening. Visits since Louise's death have, until now, seen me occupy the victim role, my needs and predicament unavoidably taking centre stage. But this time I felt Louise's absence just that little less keenly, there was other conversation, laughter, and I found myself enjoying being amongst friends for its own sake, not the therapy value.

This is not so much a lightening of the load as the beginning of an acceptance of it. I am a widower. I didn't choose this life but it has found me and I must make the best of it. I am not, by nature, a positive thinker but Louise's death is so big, so potentially destructive an event that I have come to the conclusion I must go against type and fashion as resilient and hopeful a mindset as possible. Without it I would have buckled by now.

I continue to look back, at what was, what has been lost and wonder at what might have been. But I am also tentatively beginning to look forward, towards what will be. And in doing so I am starting to understand, sometimes, that 'possibility' still exists in life. Crippled possibility but possibility nevertheless. It's still formless, I don't know what it might look like, but I know that it's there and it is down to me to give it shape and substance. I cannot change what happened that evening on 23rd January but I can influence the way in which I respond to it, whether I sink or swim.

And sinking is not an option. Louise would not allow it. She wanted me to live, prosper and find love again. She told me so in her farewell letter. It was her final gift to me, and one of her most precious. I take it as an instruction and an obligation. Achieving it will make at least some sense of an act which was otherwise entirely devoid of sense. It is a means by which I can continue to please Louise and make her proud of me. In this way of thinking I can even begin to find a degree of accommodation with the thought of a future relationship with someone other than Louise. It will be with her blessing, not an act of betrayal or infidelity but rather one which honours Louise's love and hope for me.

This emerging positivity, fragile and easily-punctured though it is liable to be, may seem curiously inconsistent with sentiments of renewed despair and hopelessness expressed barely a week ago. But the duality of mood, a tendency to oscillate, rapidly, between light and darkness is an accurate representation of where I am six months after Louise's death. I stand at something of a midway point between my old life with Louise, one which is still close enough for me to feel, to be able to reach out and touch, and a new unknown life on my own which I soon need to begin to establish. I currently belong to neither and both. But while Louise and my old life will always travel with me, I know that the direction I must eventually take is towards the future; my future.

Exhaustion

19th August | 208 days

Early on in this journey, I came to the conclusion that the overwhelming experience of bereavement wasn't loss, despair, guilt or anger but love, a love for Louise of startling purity and raw intensity. That love hasn't dimmed. I will hold it forever, Louise's most precious gift to me. But now, nearly seven months on, the overriding day-to-day sensation is perhaps different and somewhat less noble. It is exhaustion.

Grief hollows you out, both physically and mentally. I came to it already on my knees. While Louise's death was sudden and shockingly unexpected, we had together been fighting her severe depression for several months, managing the strains and pressures and the emotional distress this brought on a daily basis, the darkness pervading every aspect of our lives. During this same period, Louise had lost her father in traumatic circumstances and my mother had been cripplingly disabled by a catastrophic stroke. Neither of us had any reserves of strength left to draw on. We agreed that we wouldn't have the capacity to deal with even the smallest further crisis.

And then I found myself dealing with the largest crisis of my life.

In the early days after Louise's death, I was carried through by a cocktail of shock, numbness and a form of adrenalin. Friends and family were notified of the news, funeral arrangements were made, eulogies written, paperwork dealt with. I was rarely off the phone. The whole world, it seemed, wanted to talk to me. And I needed to talk to them. But gradually the formalities and rituals of death and commemoration were observed, the calls dried up, people returned to their lives and I was left to begin the process of coming to terms with my new reality, the grim day-to-day slog of life without Louise.

It's a wearisome journey in every respect, a supreme effort simply to maintain my composure, keep going and appear strong in public. The lack of sleep is physically punishing. Even those of us who once slept soundly find that, in grief, the facility deserts us. Four hours sleep a night is barely sustainable over seven months. It's not that I cannot sleep. In fact I am so tired it's a constant struggle to remain awake. I find myself dozing off, my head dropping and eyes closing, while I am at work and talking to family and friends. I constantly fear doing so while behind the wheel of my car. The ability to drive while exhausted is, like driving while crying, a key survival technique the newly bereaved quickly acquire.

But I will not allow myself to sleep, even when I should do so, even when my body is screaming at me to switch off. My brain is so active, processing thoughts, trying to make sense of what has happened, that it is almost impossible to stop, even in the middle of the night. My natural body clock tends towards the late shift anyway but without Louise's restraining and moderating influences, or the motivation to discipline myself, I keep going, thinking, doing, turning night into day in the process.

The emotional intensity is sapping. Imagine just one thought on your mind almost every waking moment for seven months. And it's a destructive, despairing one. Outside of work, and when I can escape into football on a Saturday afternoon, there has been barely no time since that January evening when I have stopped thinking about Louise's death or been doing something in some way connected with the consequences. The daily outbursts of tears, holding and processing the traumatic memories of the night itself and the events leading up to it, learning to live alone, trying to envisage and re-plan a future utterly different in every way to the one that I thought would be mine. And all the time, never far from the surface, the guilt and the 'if onlys' which play on a constant loop.

Then there is the seemingly never-ending bureaucracy which needs to be attended to, the process of officially closing down Louise's life, from filing her final tax returns to returning her library books. And above all the compulsion, one which I am completely unable to resist, to spend every spare moment in some kind of activity to memorialise Louise, to honour her memory and record our lives together; to write this book, my blog and diary, to use recovery software to search for hours for lost fragments of video footage, to print out email and text conversations, to digitise hard copy photos and documents and print electronic ones in the interests of secure back up.

I will not be able to rest until this process is complete, until I can be satisfied that Louise, the person and my marriage to her, is safely captured and stored for posterity in every possible way. It is the closest that I can come to keeping her alive, alongside me. This is now all I have left.

Before I returned to work, I at least had the time and space to grieve. In those initial weeks I could devote myself almost all the time to my needs. But they have long since somehow had to be fitted in around the demanding responsibilities of daily working life and supporting my partially-dependent Mother.

And when I am not working or on caring duty I have tried hard to 'do the right thing' and resist the temptation to retreat into my shell, to sit at home licking my wounds. I try to make the effort to reach out to people. Not only to maintain contact with old friends and my place in Louise's family but also to meet and interact with new people through support groups. In doing so, I am partly driven by a genuine desire to help others struggling along the same path as myself, but I am also mindful that some of my old networks, those built around Louise, will fail and I need to look for new ones if I am not to risk bitter and lonely isolation.

This unsustainable whirl of activity and thought leaves me exhausted, my head full, my nerves frayed. I yearn for a break, to be able to find the off switch but it seems not to exist. Relaxation is beyond me. I cannot watch TV or read a book. I have no interest or energy to do so and my concentration span is shot to pieces.

A holiday would be pointless. Whenever I think about the respite it might bring I realise I am chasing an illusion because my vision of a holiday is inextricably bound up in those I shared with Louise, moments and experiences that are now gone for ever. In any event, grief and loss cannot be escaped and would follow me wherever I went. Louise's absence would be as keenly felt on holiday as everywhere else, perhaps even more so since they were times when we were never parted.

It is somewhat ironic that as I find myself stabilising emotionally I realise that I am still at risk of breakdown. The difference is that now it is less likely to be from the despair of grief or the trauma of the experience than from sheer exhaustion. I urgently need rest. I need to be able to step outside the world I am trapped within, if only for a short period. I am, however, completely unable to work out how to do so.

Letting Go of Grief

29th August | 218 days

At every point in this journey through grief, I face loss. Louise's death represented not the end of the process but the beginning. The bewildering and shocking loss of her physical presence is reinforced and multiplied by hundreds, thousands, of smaller but still significant deaths. Whenever something which was part of her life – which stood as a proxy for her existence on this planet, her part in my life – disappears I mourn all over again. When I throw away her favourite food, cancel her driving licence, remove her toothbrush from the bathroom, I experience another break with the past. I take a further painful step away from the person, and the life, that I loved so much. But there is a loss which is rarely recognised as such; the loss of grief.

By this I do not mean the loss of sadness or remembrance. They will be enduring, eternal. I would not wish it to be any other way since they are a mark of the extent to which my life has been touched by Louise, proof of the love that existed between us. I will shed tears for Louise and her suffering for the rest of my life. Nor do I mean the loss of loneliness – if only that could be so easily waved goodbye. I don't even necessarily mean the loss of some of the individual raw emotions of grief: the despair, the guilt, the fear.

But I am approaching a point when I will need to have the courage to let go of the mindset of acute grief, of victimhood and exceptionalism. When I stop framing my whole life in the context of Louise's death, defining myself by my loss, identifying myself primarily as a widower. When I stop looking only over my shoulder, back towards what I had, what I have lost, or looking forward only in the terms of what I will now never have. When I stop expecting to receive preferential treatment.

I cannot carry the intensity of raw grief forever. It is not sustainable. It is too exhausting, too destabilising, too disabling. If I try, it will destroy me. I have to let light, hope and opportunity back into my life. I have to start to live again, tentatively at first no doubt, but hopefully with increasing confidence and certainty. This, to some extent, will require a conscious decision to do so, and a determined effort to maintain it. It is the use of the power of positive thinking on a grand scale.

You might think that I would embrace the loss of grief gladly, that I would be only too keen to be rid of something so dark and destructive. And, of course, I am. A few days ago, after selling the car that Louise and I shared together, that took us on so many holidays, so many visits to friends and family, and in which we enjoyed so many conversations, I again found myself prostrate, disabled by tears wondering when, or indeed whether, this nightmare will ever end, when the pain will stop and I can emerge into a gentler and more hopeful world.

But the transition from grief can, in itself, be painful and frightening. It is a form of loss in its own right. It is very easy to cling to grief like a comfort blanket. It has become a familiar part of my life over many months. In fact, it has *become* my life, my identity. Who am I? 'I am a widower'. How am I?' 'I am grieving the loss of my wife'. That's it. Nothing else about me or my life has mattered for longer than I can now easily remember.

I have become consumed by the rituals and activities of grief and memorialisation to the point where I have had no other connection with the rest of the world, no other form of conversation, and precious few other forms of thought. I have come to understand the rhythms and routines of grief. In a world where I have lost almost all my reference points, this is a form of certainty. A normality of sorts.

Grief protects me from the need to plan, to think, to act. This is convenient because I know that I am not capable of doing so. It reduces people's expectations of me to a tolerable level, one fitting to my crippled capacity. It means that I am treated gently and with respect.

And perhaps, above all else, it's easy and comforting to come to interpret my grief as evidence of my love and a sign that I continue to hold Louise in the present. For so long as I cry every day, for so long as I feel that wretched, twisting void in the pit of my stomach, for so long as I feel myself a stranger separated from the rest of the world around me by an invisible but insurmountable barrier – for so long as I hold on to grief – it's easy to prove to myself, to others and most importantly to Louise, how much I cared for her. Grief can be taken to validate love. By clinging on to emotion, I cling on to Louise. She is still here, with me, because I feel so deeply.

Letting go of all this is not easy. It means that I have to learn how to remember and honour Louise, to demonstrate my love for her, in ways which are more positive and celebratory. I have to lift my head and look towards a future that is uncertain and ill-defined. I have to find the energy to make plans, take charge of my life once more, begin to take risks in establishing the new normal, work out what feels right and what doesn't. I have to allow myself, once more, to be judged by the same standards as others and open myself to the possibility of rejection and failure. And I have to do all these things on my own.

It also means that I have to come to terms with how others see me. While close family and friends will no doubt recognise and adjust to my development and understand me for who I am, not what has happened to me, many people will continue to define me by my loss. And, as I take Louise's story out into the medical community, using the power of the personal narrative to raise funds to support the needs of doctors battling with mental illness, I will come face-to-face with those for whom the news of her death is fresh and find myself, yet again, the object of sympathy and condolences.

None of us see ourselves as tragic figures and it is a curious and potentially destabilising thing to be viewed in this way, particularly when we ourselves are trying to find a new self. I will have to learn to accept that, for many, Louise's death is what I will be known for and find a way to wear this lightly, to prevent it dragging me back into the identity of grief.

There is plenty there to frighten me. And it makes me feel guilty, as if in the process of saying goodbye to grief I am also bidding farewell to Louise. Every time I laugh, every time I find myself distracted, every time I plan an activity my conscience pulls me up: '*What do you think you're doing? Don't you realise it's only months since Louise died? How can you have forgotten already?*'

Nevertheless, I believe that I am ready to take the first faltering and imperfect steps beyond acute grief. It will not be easy and I will frequently fall back, perhaps particularly as Christmas and the anniversary in January of Louise's death approach.

But I can carry with me the confidence that I have acquired, merely by surviving these past seven months, the knowledge that however difficult it may be to learn to live again, nothing can be as challenging as what has gone before. I will not be moving on, leaving Louise behind. I will be moving forward, taking her and everything that she gave me into my new life. It is by doing this, and not by grieving, that I can most appropriately honour Louise and continue to uphold my love for her.

Breaking Down the Barriers

1st September | 221 days

The closed Facebook and web forum pages of the young widowed community are daily filled with discussions on the practical aspects of life that need to be faced when our partners have been wrenched away from us at an unexpectedly early age. And one of the perpetual themes, right up there alongside how to deal with the grief of children at the same time as our own, whether to continue to wear the wedding ring and the agonies, guilt and confusion of dating again, is how to continue to connect with friends at a time when our lives and experience diverge from them so sharply.

This is such a universal issue that there must be a common explanation for the anxieties the newly-widowed feel about the challenges of maintaining meaningful contact with friends. Our relationships become more complicated to navigate, and no wonder. We are no longer the same people. We have changed and so have our needs. Our emotional state can be disturbing, unpredictable and mystifying. It's all too easy for barriers of fear and mutual incomprehension to emerge.

In the early days of loss, we are inundated with messages of support and sympathy and offers of assistance. During this period there is some equality of shock and grief. Everybody is reeling. This shared experience brings some comfort and the task of responding to the stream of well-wishers provides a welcome, if exhausting, diversion and focus.

But friends are generally subsequently able to move on with their lives relatively quickly, their day-to-day landscape broadly unchanged, while we inevitably find ourselves left far behind, every detail of our lives transformed for the worse, trapped within the new reality, unable to escape the consequences even for a single moment and acutely conscious that the rest of the world continues to revolve without us. We want to receive help but don't know how to reach out for it. Our friends want to provide that help, to ease the hurt, but don't know how to give it and are afraid that they will say or do the wrong thing, or even lay open their own distress and, perhaps, guilt. The two parties are separated by a psychological Berlin Wall. All too often, both sides assume the other will know how to tear it down but generally neither does. As a consequence, sometimes the two end up sitting in unhappy isolation.

The needs of the bereaved are difficult for those who have not experienced close personal loss to understand or anticipate. They are complex and constantly shifting because that is the nature of grief itself. Grief is often seen in terms of a progression through stages of emotion and need until some form of normalisation is obtained. We, the bereaved, are constantly anxious that others may be measuring our mental state against some form of orthodox timescale for recovery, petrified that we will be perceived to be weak and abnormal if we haven't 'got over it' by a certain point in time.

But we know for ourselves that the reality is much less straightforward, the end point much less clear cut, and the clock by which we measure time moves much more slowly than that belonging to others. We will never 'get over' the loss of our partner but we will, in time, move to a position where we can learn to accommodate the sadness and build another life around it.

The process by which we do this, however, is not linear. It cannot be captured by any number of neat lines drawn on an explanatory graph. There *is* progression over a period of time but its course is so unpredictable and convoluted that it is often difficult to see in the moment. The path that is travelled is not on a straight line motorway but through a maze. After the initial raw shock has begun to fade, we find ourselves caught up in a maelstrom of emotions.

Nobody can grieve continuously for month after month without respite. It simply isn't psychologically sustainable. Instead, we zig zag back and forth between composure, maybe even optimism and hopelessness, and then back again once more. Lightness and darkness, hope and despair, coping and not coping can follow each other with dizzying speed, or maybe even coexist simultaneously. Periods of 'strength' and recovery can be punctuated by sudden reversals brought about by the slightest trigger of the memory or the escape of a usually suppressed line of thought. These reversals may last just hours or instead continue for days, weeks or months.

And overlaid on this confusing picture is the fact that the way in which we grieve, and the length of time for which we grieve, is dependent upon so many very personal variables; our personalities, our financial and psychological resources, the amount of support we can draw upon from family and friends, our faith and cultural norms, the nature of our domestic circumstances, the type of the relationship we had with our partner and the manner of our partner's death.

It's no wonder that even the bravest, wisest and most intuitive of our friends can feel helpless. Struggling, sometimes, to deal with their own sadness, it can be impossible to know how to reach out. What to do for the best. Sometimes we want to be surrounded by people, sometimes we need to be alone.

Sometimes we want to be drawn out of ourselves, distracted, other times we just need to have somebody sit and listen to us talk – and repeat ourselves over and over. And sometimes, when we talk, we do so about emotions and events that are uncomfortable, that are difficult to listen to, ones for which no solution can be offered.

Further, we have become so accustomed to being surrounded by the signs of death and loss that we sometimes barely notice, or take comfort in, things which others recoil from, an item of our loved one's clothing still left lying carelessly around the house perhaps, or their ashes tucked away on a shelf while we make up our minds what to do with them. To be fully able to support us, our friends must be prepared to experience and share some of our pain.

But modern society doesn't prepare people to deal with the overwhelming emotions unleashed by death. Medical advances mean that, at least in the First World, we may well reach our fifties or sixties without experiencing major loss. Death is hidden away, something exceptional. We shrink even from the word itself, preferring euphemisms kinder on our sensibilities. People don't die, they 'pass away', 'depart', or 'leave us'. We think that those advances in medical science absolve us of the need to consider death, or the consequences for those left behind. Mortality has been conquered. Except, of course, it hasn't. We may now be able to postpone death for longer but it remains as inevitable as ever.

Because no two people grieve in exactly the same way, it's difficult to give definitive advice on how best to support us, other than to make sure that people know you are there for them and not to assume that we will call for help if we need it – because we probably won't. However, the approach set out by an unknown author in the piece below which is so familiar within the widowed community, is the most insightful and accurate I have yet come across. It deserves repetition here and the widest possible audience. We can tear down those barriers but only if we learn, all of us, to more openly recognise the existence of death and talk freely about its impact on the living.

HOW YOU CAN HELP ME

Please talk about my loved one, even though she is gone. It is more comforting to cry than to pretend that she never existed. I need to talk about her, and I need to do it over and over.

Be patient with my agitation. Nothing feels secure in my world. Get comfortable with my crying. Sadness hits me in waves, and I never know when my tears may flow. Just sit with me in silence and hold my hand.

Don't abandon me with the excuse that you don't want to upset me. You can't catch my grief. My world is painful, and when you are too afraid to call me or visit or say anything, you isolate me at a time when I most need to be cared about. If you don't know what to say, just come over, give me a hug or touch my arm, and gently say, "I'm sorry." You can even say, "I just don't know what to say, but I care, and want you to know that."

Just because I look good does not mean that I feel good. Ask me how I feel only if you really have time to find out. I am not strong. I'm just numb.

When you tell me I am strong, I feel that you don't see me. I will not recover. This is not a cold or the flu. I'm not sick. I'm grieving and that's different.

My grieving may only begin 6 months after my loved one's death. Don't think that I will be over it in a year. For I am not only grieving her death, but also the person I was when I was with her, the life that we shared, the plans we had for watching our children and grandchildren grow, the places we will never get to go together, and the hopes and dreams that will never come true.

My whole world has crumbled and I will never be the same. I will not always be grieving as intensely, but I will never forget my loved one and rather than recover, I want to incorporate her life and love into the rest of my life. She is a part of me and always will be, and sometimes I will remember her with joy and other times with a tear. Both are okay. I don't have to accept the death. Yes, I have to understand that it has happened and it is real, but there are some things in life that are just not acceptable.

When you tell me what I should be doing, then I feel even more lost and alone. I feel badly enough that my loved one is dead, so please don't make it worse by telling me I'm not doing this right.

Please don't tell me I can find someone else or that I need to start dating again. I'm not ready. And maybe I don't want to. And besides, what makes you think people are replaceable? They aren't. Whoever comes after will always be someone different.

I don't even understand what you mean when you say, "You've got to get on with your life." My life is going on, I've been forced to take on many new responsibilities and roles. It may not look the way you think it should. This will take time and I will never be my old self again. So please, just love me as I am today, and know that with your love and support, the joy will slowly return to my life. But I will never forget and there will always be times that I cry.

I need to know that you care about me. I need to feel your touch, your hugs. I need you just to be with me, and I need to be with you.

I need to know you believe in me and in my ability to get through my grief in my own way, and in my own time.

Please don't say, "Call me if you need anything." I'll never call you because I have no idea what I need. Trying to figure out what you could do for me takes more energy than I have. So, in advance, let me give you some ideas:

(a) Bring food or a film over to watch together.

(b) Send me a card on special holidays, her birthday, and the anniversary of her death, and be sure to mention her name. You can't make me cry. The tears are here and I will love you for giving me the opportunity to shed them because someone cared enough about me to reach out on this difficult day.

(c) Ask me more than once to join you at a film or lunch or dinner. I may say no at first or even for a while, but please don't give up on me because somewhere down the line, I may be ready, and if you've given up then I really will be alone.

(d) Understand how difficult it is for me to be surrounded by couples, to walk into events alone, to go home alone, to feel out of place in the same situations where I used to feel so comfortable.

Please don't judge me now - or think that I'm behaving strangely. Remember I'm grieving. I may even be in shock. I am afraid. I may feel deep rage. I may even feel guilty. But above all, I hurt. I'm experiencing a pain unlike any I've ever felt before and one that can't be imagined by anyone who has not walked in my shoes.

Don't worry if you think I'm getting better and then suddenly I seem to slip backward. Grief makes me behave this way at times.
And please don't tell me you know how I feel, or that it's time for me to get on with my life. What I need now is time to grieve.

Most of all thank you for being my friend. Thank you for your patience. Thank you for caring. Thank you for helping, for understanding. Thank you for praying for me. And remember in the days or years ahead, after your loss - when you need me as I have needed you - I will understand. And then I will come and be with you.

Help Along the WAY

5th September | 225 days

An image sprang into my mind the other day. It was of one of the iconic pieces of Great War film footage so often replayed on television; grainy and rudimentary newsreel coverage of injured troops, all of them blinded, marching unsteadily, their hands outstretched holding on to the shoulder of their comrade in front. None of them could see but despite their incapacity they were each able to help others suffering similarly. And by this means everybody was able to make the same journey along the road to safety. It struck me that there were parallels to be drawn with the young widowed community, a group of vulnerable, grieving but immensely resilient men and women groggily but generously helping each other through the most shattering of experiences.

Like most of us, I have become accustomed to turning to the internet for the answers to problems in life. It can help me fix a broken boiler, find the best savings rates, and provide me with directions to pretty much anywhere. It was even the means by which Louise and I met. So, in the early hours of the morning a few days after she died I naturally found myself looking online for assistance with my response to the most shattering event of my life. But this time my expectations were rock bottom. Googling 'help for young widowers' wasn't going to be able to bring Louise back so what could possibly come of it? The answer was WAY Widowed and Young, which describes itself as a peer to peer support group for men and women aged 50 or under when their partner died. I prefer to describe it as my lifeline.

It is not normal to suffer the loss of your partner before you have even fully adjusted to the concept of middle age. Family and friends attempt to offer support but it's unlikely that any have even a remotely comparable experience to fall back on. I am the first in my circles to lose my wife. Few amongst my friends, thankfully, have yet even experienced the death of a parent. For many, Louise's death was itself the closest they have been touched by personal loss.

People tried to do the right thing, reach for the right words. I am immensely grateful for the support and kindness shown by so many. But they knew as well as I did that they couldn't possibly fully understand. They could not really know how it was for me. I was alone not just in the immensity of my loss but also in the whole experience. I didn't have the words to begin to explain the maelstrom of emotions and the thoughts catapulting around inside my head. I desperately needed to find people who had trodden the same path, who understood. Acutely aware of how exceptional my circumstances were, I felt something of a freak, the object of sympathy, concern, pity and countless conversations.

The first time that I walked into a pub full of widows and widowers, some eight weeks on, I therefore came close to bursting into tears of relief. It still felt odd to be associating myself with the terms 'widow' and 'widower', words which conjure up visions of sour elderly ladies dressed in black and sad old men whiling away their time sitting on park benches. But these members of the local WAY group were remarkable only for their normality, indistinguishable from any other group out for a Friday evening drink. They were the same as me. Evidently being a widower did not have to mark you out.

Even better, I immediately discovered the commonality of experience between us. We may come from all walks of life and we may all respond to grief in different ways, influenced by the many variables derived from our individual characters and the circumstances of our loss, but the basic human emotions in bereavement are universal and the practical challenges faced by young widows often the same.

I therefore suddenly found myself surrounded by people who 'got it'. Here I was normal. Here I found myself needing to explain less, since understanding came instinctively. Here I could smile and laugh without fear of people misunderstanding how difficult things really were. Here I had nobody telling me I was brave when I knew that all I was doing was trying to get on with my life. Here I heard people voicing my own pain, fears and distress. Here I was surrounded by people who knew exactly how difficult it would be to part at the end of the evening and return home to dark, echoing, empty houses.

I continue to rely on this community to get me through. While there are frequent social events and activities and private real world friendships also develop, much of the support is inevitably virtual. A day never passes without contact with my peers through the online forums. These are places where you can seek advice on everything from procedures at inquests to the perils of navigating new relationships, where you can obtain reassurance that your wild emotions, dark thoughts and irrational coping behaviours are perfectly normal, where those who have children discuss how to cope as single parents, where you learn to count your blessings when you encounter those whose situation is even more difficult than your own and where you can go at the end of the day and express the small injustices, irritations and victories of daily life that previously we would have shared with our partners over the dinner table.

Perhaps most importantly, however, the forums are places where you can cry out in pain in the middle of the night and know that there will be an instant response from those who are on the same journey and where you can draw comfort and hope from the encouragement and example of those further down that road.

It is here that I draw the parallel with the image of those injured soldiers. For every person within this community is struggling with their own grief, loneliness and exhaustion. Yet everybody gives generously of their time, devotes some of their precious reserves of strength to listen, encourage, guide and support others, many of whom they have never met and will never meet. And they do so in the knowledge that when they too need a helping hand it will be quickly offered in return.

It is not a world that you want to have the need to belong to in the first instance. It may not be one in which you have a need to linger in any longer than is necessary to prepare you for a return to something approaching a normal life. But in the moment of need it is practical, uplifting and a source of never-ending inspiration.

Louise, who was a passionate believer in the power and virtues of community and constantly sought it in her daily life, would be thrilled to know that it is doing more than anything to help me heal.

Standstill

13th September | 233 days

I've been kidding myself in recent weeks. Proud of my strength and resilience I had begun to believe that I had mastered grief, that I was exempt from the setbacks and continuing struggles experienced by others. I was beginning to find living tolerable again and, trying hard to think positively, even to sense hope and opportunity. I know the theory. I've read the books, talked at length to those further on in this journey than myself. I should have known better. Grief might temporarily relax its hold but it doesn't give it up that easily. It merely changes its grip, alters its character.

This is quite different in nature from the early days, not the violent paroxysms of emotional distress, despair and hopelessness. It's less dramatic but nearly as debilitating and more entrenched. I've simply come to a standstill. The accumulated impact of carrying the grief for nearly eight months, the emotional and physical strain, has finally worn me down to the point where I feel as though I can go no further. My reserves of strength have been exhausted.

I thought that I knew true tiredness before… but I was mistaken. Both my mind and body feel as though they are shutting down. I have no energy or motivation even to perform the simplest of tasks – getting out of bed on a morning, never something which came easily to me, is now the biggest single challenge of the day. Earlier this week I was so tired that I overslept the alarm clock and woke to find that I had already missed most of the morning at work. What had previously seemed to be a relatively orderly progression towards recovery and the establishment of a normal – if different – lifestyle suddenly began to feel chaotic.

For the first time in months I have begun to question my complacent pride in my progress. Louise and I had no children. I therefore do not possess the clear motivation, the essential need, to maintain structures, routine and self-discipline that those widowed with young children are likely to. Instead, my inspiration, the source from which I draw the strength to keep going and to work towards recovery, is Louise herself. She was always incredibly proud of me. I could never quite work out why. I am not very remarkable. But however undeserved it may have been, I drank that pride in like the purest nectar. When Louise told me that she loved me I felt good. When she told me that she was proud of me, it felt like nothing I have ever before experienced. So the thought now of letting her down, of not coping, is crushing.

One of the reasons why Louise took her life was because, in the confusion of her mind at that time, she thought she was releasing me to have a better future. If I remain locked in my own struggles, if I am unable to go on to build a new and rewarding life, her sacrifice will somehow seem even more ridiculously wasteful than it already does. I must come through this for Louise's sake. It's the only way that I can possibly make any sense of such an utterly bewildering act.

Yet I seem to be going backwards. Six weeks ago, I felt that I was coming close to a return to my normal capacity at work. Now my concentration span is once more shredded and my function significantly impaired. The toilet cubicles are again a place of refuge, though this time not to hide my tears but to allow me to close my eyes for five minutes, to snatch enough half-sleep to keep me going for another hour or two.

The stress is beginning to have a physical manifestation beyond mere tiredness. The night sweats may have stopped but my long dormant hypochondria is running riot. Worries about my physical health and the strains of a difficult domestic issue have tipped the balance from coping to not coping. And there is always the lack of sleep, my inability to properly manage my routines and sleep patterns, to impose structure and order. I go to bed in the middle of the night. At weekends I get up in the middle of the day. During the week I just get up without sleep.

I should be better than this. I do not like the exhausted and chaotic person I have become. And I am scared of the potential consequences if I continue on the same path; the risk of inadvertent self-harm through accident, or of psychological damage.

To my enormous relief I have, so far, been spared the visions and flashbacks so many warned me of. I pass the spot in the house where I found Louise's body dozens of times every day. The open plan nature of our house means that it is almost never out of sight whenever I am downstairs. Even the most mundane of daily activities trigger direct memories and associations. Every time that I open the fridge I find myself standing exactly where I did that night. So far I have handled this much more easily than I would have thought possible, but I remain constantly frightened of once again seeing Louise as I did then. It would not just be emotionally devastating but would also, surely, force me out of my home. Emotional and physical exhaustion must make this possibility more likely.

The temptation is to retreat into myself. To take time off work, pull up the drawbridge and curl up in a corner to rest and lick my wounds. But there is danger in this. Work provides structure and distraction and offers some form of validation and an alternative purpose. It would be too easy to find myself at home, isolated, wallowing in introspection. I have kept going over the months through the force of momentum. If I stop, I may not find it easy to start again. If I do step back briefly to try and refresh myself I must therefore retain a focus and keep active.

As I write these words I am forcibly struck by the parallels with Louise's dilemma as she struggled unsuccessfully to cope with the emptiness of time while off work during her last days, beset by the bleakest of outlooks and the darkest of thoughts with nothing to offer uplifting diversion. The challenges facing me are, in some respects, similar.

But the parallels stop there. I am not mentally ill, I am tired and grieving. This is my lowest point for a while but I know that it is merely a diversion on the road to recovery. I have already come a long way and briefly glimpsed the hope and possibility that are waiting for me. I continue to believe in their existence. I can still make Louise proud of me.

The Bravest Act

19th September | 239 days

Louise was normally a confident passenger, happy to sleep while I was driving long distances. But on this occasion she couldn't settle and sat watching the road ahead anxiously. It was 2am and we were driving a strange hire car in the dark on unfamiliar Sicilian motorways, returning to our holiday villa a couple of hours south after a long, happy but tiring daytrip to Mount Etna and the chic resort of Taormina. I was tired, feeling unwell and driving on the 'wrong' side of the road. Louise was alert to the risk of an accident. Three months before she took her life her will to live, her instinctive desire for survival was strong. This was not somebody who treated life carelessly. She valued it and did not want to die.

Before I met Louise, my attitudes towards mental illness and suicide were probably typical of those of the population at large; they were signs of weakness, a deficiency in character. I probably even fell back on the tired old cliché that sufferers simply needed to exercise a degree of resolve and 'pull themselves together'. While many people were enduring 'real' physical ailments, I could find within myself little patience or understanding for something as complex and intangible as a troubled mind. Only the vulnerable and needy experienced mental ill health. Suicide was a form of cowardice.

Nothing, I now know, could be further from the truth. Louise was as far removed from my antediluvian stereotype as it is possible to be. Independent, resourceful and a natural optimist, she loved life with a passion which put most of us to shame and lived it every day with a glorious, inspiring sense of hope, opportunity, generosity and vigour. Louise was, quite simply, the happiest person that I have ever met. She would frequently cuddle up to me at night and simply declare 'I'm so happy'. The light in her eyes did not lie.

But neither did it tell the whole story. For unknown to all but those close to her, Louise suffered periodically from anxiety and depression throughout her adult life. At the age of barely 18, she demonstrated remarkable insight and maturity when describing something of this state of mind in a school leavers' booklet so acutely that it was instantly recognisable to me when it was brought to my attention after her death, 22 years later.

To battle a debilitating darkness of mind for a lifetime is extraordinarily exhausting and requires incredible bravery just to summon up the strength and the will to keep going. I saw the daily struggle during those periods when

Louise was unwell, when her head was, as she described it, so 'full' of a cacophony of destructive and doubting thoughts that it was impossible for her to escape, to switch off.

I saw how much energy this consumed, how it corroded self-belief and led to uncertainty, indecision and restlessness. I saw and admired Louise's openness and honesty in confronting the illness and the way in which she sought to take responsibility for it and identified and pursued means of throwing it off. I came to understand how little a part reason or logic could play in soothing such troubles, the futility of rationalisation. I came to learn that mental illness is as real, insidious and dangerous as any other, one that sufferers have no more control over than they would cancer or multiple sclerosis.

And I came to be in awe of Louise's resilience and fortitude, not only in enduring the illness but fighting back, never allowing it to define or limit her. To be the person that Louise was, to achieve what she did both professionally and personally, even had she been completely well at all times, would have made her very special. But to do it all despite the recurring illness made her quite remarkable.

That same bravery followed Louise right to the very end. I know, both from conversations beforehand and the content of her farewell letter, that Louise saw what she was doing as a pragmatic answer to her mental torment. In her muddled thinking at the time she also looked upon it as a means of releasing me from the stress and challenge of a wife with mental illness.

Louise had enough spirit and tenacity to fight the darkness hard, right up to the very last moments. As that episode in Sicily illustrated, her survival instincts remained strong. She didn't want to die and had no comforting vision or expectation of an afterlife to fall back on – her Christianity always focused on the grace in this life. But having identified what seemed to be a practical solution she acted on it for her sake and, as she thought, for mine. Here I have to split my mind in two. There is no romance or redemption in suicide. It is always messy and tragically wasteful. It leaves loved ones with unique emotional scars. I still cannot easily fully describe what I witnessed. Not because I lack the words but because I am afraid of setting the tightly-held memory free to roam. Despite the fact that I understand why Louise was driven to take her life, where the bleakness of thought and outlook had led her, and that I understand it was not an act of free will because of the malign power exerted by the illness, I am still taunted by the cruel needlessness of it.

Nevertheless, it is possible, even while loathing the act and the shattering consequences, to recognise the logic that sat behind Louise's decision and the incredible courage, generosity and determination it must have taken to arrive at this point and then follow her thought processes through.

We tend not to think of suicide as a rational act. Even here I have talked of Louise's confusion and muddled thinking. But rationality is the luxury of a healthy mind. Those of us who have been fortunate enough to avoid the grip of darkness are in no real position to sit in judgment on what makes sense from deep within it. Oblivion must appear to be at the very least a viable alternative to life when you are so tortured, know that you have been tortured in the past, and believe that you will go on to experience the same torture over and over again in the future.

Within the context of her illness *as it was affecting her at that moment in time*, Louise's desire for escape from the pain was no different to that of somebody with a severe disability who seeks a form of assisted dying. The tragedy came in the temporary nature of that pain, the certainty of eventual respite if she had only been able to hold on a little longer.

But regardless of however wrong and misguided we – who are well – can see the act to have been, it was a far braver and more selfless thing than I or most of us would ever be capable of. The easy option would have been to continue to try to muddle through but, as always, Louise went a step beyond, to do what she thought was necessary and right. And typically, even in the midst of her distress, she was thinking of others, applying herself to what, in her mind, was the best outcome for me and attempting in her last moments to protect me from its immediate impact.

Louise was not, therefore, guilty of weakness, cowardice or selfishness. On the contrary, she was the strongest and most giving person I have ever been privileged to know. Her determination in her long battle against mental illness and her monumental courage to follow through with such a drastic solution are testament to her remarkable character. Louise died in the manner in which she lived: courageously, practically and imbued with love and generosity of spirit. Her only fault, it turned out, was that ultimately she was too brave.

A Letter on our Special Day

24th September | 244 days

I haven't written to you Sweetheart since my reply to your farewell letter. The tear-soaked one that I somehow managed to read out to you while sitting next to your coffin in the undertakers, stroking your hair for the last time. The one that accompanied you on your final journey. I haven't really needed to write. I can talk to you at any time, no matter where I am. But today is special. This time four years ago we were walking on the clouds. It was the happiest moment of our lives. The day that we became man and wife. Our East End wedding.

Do you remember how you were literally shaking with nerves as we stood at the altar? How overwhelmed we were by the ovation we received from nearly 200 of our family and friends as we walked hand-in-hand into the reception? How we were so busy kissing that we barely noticed my Best Man burning himself as he tried to light the candles on the cake right next to us? How everybody, without exception, told us it was the best wedding they had ever attended?

I spent every moment of that day reminding myself to savour everything, to remember every last detail. I thought that it would be a day we would recall together for the next 40 years. As we danced that night away (well okay, you danced, I stood and swayed with you) never, in my worst nightmare, could I have imagined that less than three-and-a-half years later the photos of that day which we displayed with such pride would be the backdrop to your death. That I would be returning to the wedding guest list spreadsheet we created in order to invite people to your funeral. That everybody, without exception, would soon be telling me that yours was the best memorial service they had ever attended.

Now all my carefully nurtured memories of the day are darkened by the shadow of what was to come so soon afterwards. Every picture of your gorgeous smiling face, the very definition of life and joy, shocks me, leaves me gasping for breath as I try to understand yet again how it can be that something so precious to me, so familiar to me as you no longer even exists in bodily form. I'm not sure that I can even grasp the concept of what those words mean. No. Longer. Exists.

I have been dreading this day for months. It is one of the anniversaries that stand like formidable roadblocks on the route through grief. I have watched it approach helplessly, unable to alter the course of the calendar. The date has become invested with far more significance than we ever gave it when you were alive. The need to remember is so much greater when it is all you have left.

But, in fact, memories are not all I have left. I am still blessed by the profound way in which you changed me, made me a better person. You gave me confidence in myself, stretched me, challenged me, helped me to understand my own needs, taught me compassion, the need to hear others and to avoid judgement, enabled me to appreciate the wonderful natural world around us, to glory in the joyful possibilities of life and to see the beauty in everybody, even where most see none.

I still have the gift of your friends and family who have become my friends and family. And, most, of all I still have our love for each other. Mere absence, even through death, isn't strong enough to eradicate that. It still nurtures me, sustains me. The grief which I have endured over these eight long months, a period which feels more like eight years, is in itself an expression and a consequence of that love. All the indescribable sadness which I have borne and will continue to bear to the end of my own days is a price worth paying for the privilege of knowing the joy and strength of our bond.

It would be wholly wrong to come to fear this most special of days in the years to come. I am determined that it will remain an occasion to celebrate our love and our enduring marriage. The one wedding vow which we barely noticed at the time, the one that added the caveat 'Till death us do part' may now cause me so much anguish but I disregard the meaning behind it. Nobody suggests that siblings or parents and children cease to be related upon death and so it is nonsense to suggest that we cease to be married. We remain husband and wife. There was no divorce settlement, no loss of feeling. We simply happen to be physically separated by circumstance.

It may be that I will eventually find happiness again with somebody else but there is no contradiction in this. It is something which I know you fervently hope for me. The human heart has no limit on its capacity for love and you will be held no less tightly. I promise that you will never be left behind. You will come with me into that relationship, your values will continue to guide me, your memory will continue to be honoured. My love for you will endure. As your husband, I will forever be both the luckiest and proudest man in the world.

Sweetheart, I am *still* yours. You are *still* mine. We are *still* One.

Disconnection

28th September | 248 days

I'm a white Anglo Saxon male, university educated, middle-aged, middle(ish) class. Society is apparently designed in my image. I am not a member of any of those groups which the tabloid press seek to demonise as 'other'. I belong. Or rather, I used to. Now I'm an outsider. I no longer fit. My relationship to the world around me has fundamentally changed since Louise's death.

If the past is another country then so is bereavement. I have become acutely aware of the extent to which I feel a separation from the normal daily life which continues around me. I sit on trains and pass through town centre crowds observing those around me much more keenly than before, taking in every laugh, smile and conversation overheard. Normal conversations. People discussing with their partners what they are going to have for tea, what they are going to do at the weekend. Mundane, everyday, and yet deeply precious. All this would previously have passed me by but now it serves to emphasise the extent to which I am excluded from this life.

I have passed no border controls but it feels as though I am in an alien land. I no longer connect with people's language or their emotions. What is this happiness or contentment that everybody around me seems to enjoy? I find that there are periods when I can pass for a native but something always finds me out. The sight of a couple holding hands or casually kissing each other goodbye, the sound of excited chatter about a forthcoming wedding, holiday, or night out is enough to return me to my own world of sadness, deeply jealous of anybody who has what I once had and thought was mine for the rest of my life.

I am resentful of every couple that I see, of all ages. I envy young couples for enjoying the time together that Louise and I, who met slightly later in life, never had; couples in their 30's and 40s for the time that we once had; older couples for the time that we will never have. Worse, the lack of appreciation of the gift of a loving partner betrayed in critical or disrespectful remarks about a husband or wife leaves me angry, contemptuous even. Why do these people not understand how precious it is to have a partner who is alive? Why did this have to happen to Louise and I, who were so respectful towards each other and our marriage, when there are others who are apparently so careless about their relationships?

Shamefully, sometimes, I even find myself jealous of my compatriots who exist within the hidden sub-culture of support groups for young widows, those who enjoyed longer periods with their partners than the four-and-a-half years Louise and I had together. 10 or even 15 years of marriage is very little by the standards of most but an unimaginably long time to me. I catch myself trying to bargain with God, wondering what I would trade, how many years of my own life I would offer up in order to have been able to enjoy that time with Louise.

But by the same token I am conscious too that I have reason to be grateful for the time we were able to enjoy together. Too many others, those who married at the very end, or didn't have time to marry at all, will understandably cast similarly envious eyes at me. Do I rail against the fates for the short time Louise and I were together or give thanks for being able to enjoy it at all?

I don't even really know what is happening in this strange country any longer. I have been disengaged from the news and popular culture for so long now that much of it is a mystery to me. Previously a news and politics junkie, sometimes I'm now surprised to hear of a major event that happened months ago and completely passed me by. My world has shrunk and turned almost entirely inwards. I look out of the window from time to time but with little interest or enthusiasm and always quickly return to my preoccupations: Louise, me, our past together, my future alone.

I have come to divide society into the bereaved and the non-bereaved. The world appears to be shaped for the latter, and especially those living as part of a couple. People do things in twos and I am now one. The social invitations that I would have received as part of a couple with Louise have largely dried up. I am that awkward leftover.

The media and advertisers that make us feel so inadequate as they project sanitised, idealised images of family life back onto our messy, muddled realities scarcely acknowledge the existence of the widowed. I am subjected to single supplements in hotels, a less advantageous tax regime and, where it happens to be financially beneficial to declare my single status, the suspicion of officialdom. None of these things in themselves are more than irritants, but collectively they contribute to the sense that I am now an oddity, beyond the mainstream.

I no longer fully understand the non-bereaved and they no longer fully understand me. They try hard to make contact, to say the right things, but they can't properly grasp my new environment any more than I can connect with their reality. When our respective worlds collide, things seem to jar.

Maybe this is more my fault than theirs. I have normalised my experience. It's an essential part of my healing process. I can't possibly define either Louise or myself as abnormal or our story in any way tragic. That way lays collapse into self-pity and unhealthy entitlement. My wife took her life at 40. It's my reality, my normal. I know no different. It happens to everybody, doesn't it? In my inverted world it is those who have not been bereaved, who still, inconceivably, have partners who are alive that appear exceptional. Surrounding myself with other widows and widowers in the peer support groups serves to reinforce this protective but delusional veneer.

And such is the muddle and disorientation of grief; at the same time as feeling dislocated because of this normality I also feel a sense of detachment from people's reactions to me because that same normality feels completely unreal. This would appear to be contradictory. How can something simultaneously both be entirely normal and everyday and yet also utterly unreal?

But the end result is the same. Both responses lead to a form of disconnection with those around me. On the one hand I cannot relate to the experience of others because my everyday landscape, formed as it is out of grief, loss and loneliness, is so different to theirs. But on the other hand, even when they try to reach out and empathise with my experience I still cannot connect because I find it hard to recognise as my own.

I am therefore constantly taken aback by the reaction that news of my circumstances generates. The hushed tones and sympathetic looks confuse and embarrass me. They have me shifting uncomfortably, uncertain how to deal with it all. Do they really mean me?

This was exemplified a few weeks ago after I spoke about Louise at a conference dealing with mental illness in the medical profession. When I finished there was no applause. Instead, the roomful of psychiatrists, psychologists and doctors, all hardened professionals in the field, sat for more than a minute in a silence broken only by muffled sobs and the rustling of tissues. They looked at me in pity and eventually thanked me for my courage and strength. And I looked back at them blankly, utterly bewildered that I was the cause of this reaction and the recipient of this sympathy. What courage? What strength?

In their kindness and instinctive human response, my audience thought that it was empathising with me. Instead their reaction served only to distance themselves from me. If only they had known that I was on automatic pilot and felt little of the emotion they were projecting onto me. I was telling a story, and presumably telling it well, but it didn't feel like mine. My own words were harmless, denuded of all significance by their constant repetition and my distance from their real meaning. It was my audience's reaction which upset me, caused me to consider afresh the tragedy that has occurred.

I suppose that I shall, eventually, find a way back into the mainstream. Even now, as the acute pain begins to subside, I am finding it easier to bear – if not yet relate to – the background chatter of other happier lives. I will once more get caught up in the banal everyday routine of life and find excitement and pleasure. I will feel able to socialise with the non-bereaved as well as other widows and widowers.

Maybe one day I will even get to experience life as part of a couple again, perhaps in turn to be stared at enviously and uncomprehendingly by another widow trapped the wrong side of the glass partition which separates the recently bereaved from the rest. And as time goes by, fewer and fewer people will come to my story fresh. They will either already know or have no need to know and I will be able to escape from the disconcerting sympathy and concern, the suffocating sense of exceptionalism.

But when I regain my citizenship, I hope that I can remain a dual national, able not only to fully engage with life as most others know it but also to retain something of the perspective that comes from the rupture with that world that is brought about by bereavement.

I hope that it will enable me to appreciate the small everyday pleasures and privileges of life all the more and prevent me from wasting my time and emotion on petty jealousies and frustrations. I hope that I will continue to value – above all else – the beauty of a committed and loving relationship between two people, never to run the risk of taking such a thing for granted. And I hope that the twin coping mechanisms that shield me from the very worst of the impact of Louise's death – the normalisation of my experience and the separation from it – continue to soothe and sustain me to the point where I can attain acceptance.

I will belong once more, but never in quite the same way again.

Changing Seasons

7th October | 257 days

I remember the snow so vividly. I had been waiting impatiently for it all winter and now, as I stood in the middle of the road outside the house listening to the approaching emergency sirens draw ever closer, I noticed it had finally arrived. Just the lightest of flurries but nonetheless beautiful and mesmerising as it fell gently and silently. Even in the very moment that my world was falling apart I somehow managed to register the irony that it should do so in conditions which on any other occasion, on any other day, would have given me so much pleasure.

I used to love autumn and winter. The magical October and November hues of yellow, brown and red, crisp frosty mornings and the prospect of my favourite time of year, Christmas, to look forward to. But most of all it was the cosy nights indoors, the curtains drawn, the central heating on, safely protected from the cold and darkness outside. There was almost a womb-like sense of security and comfort which became even more marked once I met Louise and our shared home was filled too with her warmth, love, and companionship. I could never understand why others struggled with winter. It was my time of year. I even proposed to Louise in two feet of snow in Berlin's Tiergarten. This year, however, the onset of the shorter, darker days fills me with apprehension.

I have been watching the markers ever since Midsummers Day, acutely aware that the return of the dark days of winter will bring with it a heightened sense of connection with that January night Louise took her life and every certainty I knew was swept away. Somehow I felt myself in something of a protective bubble during the summer. The sights, sounds, smells and rhythm of the days were sufficiently different from those of winter to enable me to feel some measure of escape from the memories and associations. The hours of darkness, the period when I am most likely to feel isolated and insecure, when my mind is liable to conjure up fears of chilling visions and flashbacks, were mercifully short.

The summer has also enabled me to stop dreading the period between 5-9pm on Fridays, the hours covering the time during which Louise died and I returned home from work to find her body. There will always now be something of a shadow, a sense of disquiet, over a point which as the end of the working week used to be a time to relish. But the light and warmth of June, July and August were so different from the darkness and cold of January that the association with place and time faded.

Now, however, the inexorable rotation of the earth is steadily bringing me back to where I started. I notice the days growing shorter and the temperatures falling. Summer has left me behind. Things are beginning to feel more and more like that darkest of nights.

When I find myself almost alone in the office on an evening with darkness reigning outside, I am taken back to those moments when fear began to grip me, slowly at first but ever more tightly as my texts and phone calls continued to go unanswered and the first pin prick of suspicion turned into panicky realisation. Every time I drive home through the darkened streets, I remember that gut-wrenching journey back from work, fearing the worst but clinging on to the hope of an innocent explanation. Every time I turn into the road I remember what it was like to see the house lit up in such an unusual way that I instantly knew those fears had been realised.

And every time that I stand outside the house fumbling for the door keys I remember the horror of those desperate moments trying to break in through the locked door, but already knowing what I was going to find, knowing that I was too late.

The shorter days don't just re-awaken memory. They heighten my already acute sense of isolation. Life retreats indoors, away from the public space. The curtains drawn, I am more thoroughly cut off from the rest of the world, left entirely to myself in an empty house with just my thoughts, recollections and fears to occupy myself until the following morning. I flood the house with light to banish the shadows, turn up the music and hunker down as best as I can. But it's a poor substitute for the warmth, brightness and activity of summer where the sights and sounds of the outside world – children playing, lawns being mown, ice cream vans chiming on their rounds – penetrated the house and offered comfort, reassurance and a sense of connection. The same internal world that once provided cosy security now feels more like a prison cell.

Winter also brings with it the indignity of the hot water bottle at night, as sure a sign of the emptiness of the bed as anything. It still means Christmas, but the significance of it has been transformed. The holiday now looms like an unwelcome reminder of infinitely happier times past. Whereas I would normally be eagerly planning how best to celebrate the occasion, now I am focusing on how to avoid it, looking for diversionary activities. And above all, winter means the anniversary of Louise's death and the build up to it, days which will inevitably bring the events back into the sharpest of focus.

But I remind myself that I can and will deal with each of these things. If nothing else, sudden bereavement and widowhood have served to transform my confidence in my resilience, recalibrated my notion of what difficult means.

I have faced the very worst that life can throw at me and am still standing, unsteadily at times but with increasing sure-footedness. And this is no longer the very worst. That is already behind me. If last winter was an earthquake, the challenges presented this time round are more in the nature of aftershocks, uncomfortable reminders of catastrophe rather than a re-run of it. Already the first few days of truly autumnal weather suggest that the anticipation may be worse than the reality. There will still be beauty in the season. I will just have to experience it alone.

Digital Memories

15th October | 265 days

I'm nearly nine months into this journey. I'm proud of the progress that I have made and confidently reassure the newly widowed that by this point the excruciating raw pain of the first weeks and months has been replaced by an all-pervading undertone of sadness which by the standards of what we have already navigated is altogether easier to live with. And yet today I found myself broken in two again.

It was my own fault. Feeling strong, I finally plucked up the courage to view a video of Louise that a friend emailed me some days ago. It's one of the better ones that I have come across, 30 seconds of her constantly in shot, playing with our friend's child. It was taken less than a year before we met so this was the Louise that I know and ache for. Everything about her was so familiar: her voice, her laugh, her movements. Even the rain mac that she was wearing (it *was* a Northumberland summer after all). Somehow the mac was particularly important. It's in the hall cupboard just feet away from me as I write this, a tangible link between that moment and now.

There was a momentary rush of joy as once more I could see and hear Louise. I could almost touch her. But I couldn't reach. Cruelly taunted by such a vivid reminder of what had so recently been, my stomach convulsed, I felt as though I'd been speared. Hours later it was still churning. Two worlds had collided. The one without Louise that I am trying to accustom myself to, and the old one. I can't reconcile them. How can Louise possibly be gone when she is still so close?

The ability of modern technology to carry us so readily and convincingly back into the past is perhaps as much a curse as a blessing at this time. While I initially drew enormous comfort from photos and video of Louise, I now find them too painful to contemplate. I try to avoid looking at the pictures of her I rushed to place on the walls. Every time I glance at my phone, I scroll beyond the home screen as quickly as possible, averting my gaze until Louise is no longer looking me in the face, smiling back at me, blessedly unaware of what life had in store for her.

I cannot bring myself to linger on my Facebook page, confronted as I am by the last proper photo of Louise that I took, her gentle, warm eyes fixed good-humouredly on mine as she patiently posed on the steps of Modica Cathedral on the last evening of our last holiday, just 72 hours before her father took his life and our world began to collapse.

Perhaps when these prompts were not so readily available it was easier for the bereaved to deal with their memories, to place them in a proper context, to allow the past to settle and truly become the past. It's too easy for us to confuse ourselves, to muddle now with then at a time when we are already struggling to separate the two.

And yet I continue to chase these memories.

I have countless lovely photos, for which I am exceedingly grateful. My love of photography and my love of Louise happily coincided and I was never more content than when I was taking pictures of her. But however artfully posed they may have been, they don't capture the essence of her. They can't bring her to life quite as vividly as the moving images and sound which I crave.

In a world where smartphones with video capability are so ubiquitous, carried almost by everybody and used everywhere, where people seem to routinely record every moment of their lives on video, it's strange that I have so little of Louise's movement and speech recorded. We probably weren't quite the generation to think to do so. The typical 11-year-old has probably captured more of the life of their school friends on video than I did of Louise. Ironically, I realised the omission, but too late. As that last holiday ended I reflected that in future I needed to remember to take video of Louise as well as photos.

There isn't a day that goes by when I don't bitterly regret the lost opportunities to do so. I have devoted hours on end to trawling phones and laptops with recovery software, hunting desperately for discarded fragments of video, rejected at the time for being of no consequence but now so precious. We didn't even have our wedding filmed, assuming, wrongly as it turned out, that there would be plenty of video shot by family and friends. I have a total of 4 minutes 23 seconds of footage of the day across a handful of short poor quality recordings. I know this so precisely because every single second counts. Yet there is a treasure trove from which I recoil. Lengthy videos of one-to-one tutorials that Louise gave to junior GPs, taken for training purposes. While these were not shared moments, and Louise was acting in her professional capacity, a side of her which I rarely saw, I have yet to be able to bring myself to look at them. I can't afford to unlock the memories and emotions they would evoke. I want to look back but know that I mustn't.

There is a sense in which I have to deny myself these excruciatingly vivid reminders if I am to continue to move forward. It is enough at present to know that they exist, to take comfort from the fact that my memory of Louise can always be replenished if I feel it slipping away.

But if I allow myself to dwell too long in the past, I risk becoming trapped there and it is no place for me now. Those memories are all it holds. One day I will be able to visit it again, but for the moment the instinct which turns me away from the photos and film serves a real purpose. It helps me to adjust my focus and live in my new reality. Not for the first time, I marvel at the way in which so many of our natural responses to grief guide and protect us along the journey.

Beginnings and Transitions

16th October | 266 days

It's not often that I compare myself to a Roman God. In fact I am reasonably certain that I've never done so before, nor will I ever do so again. But at this particular moment in time there is something of a connection to a classical deity, albeit a rather unheroic one.

Just like Janus, the God of beginnings and transitions who looked simultaneously to both past and future, I increasingly find myself with a foot in both worlds. Since Louise's death I have focused almost entirely on the past. Insofar as I have thought of the future at all it was only in terms of what has been lost, the future that I can no longer have.

But while I remain partly trapped within these memories, still mourning Louise's absence, and will no doubt continue to do so for the rest of my days, I have reached a point on this journey where I am also able to, indeed need to, lift my head and look forward. I am beginning to devote more and more time to thinking about the future that I can *still* have. I am starting to work on the blank canvas that is the rest of my life.

Less than a year ago, the pattern of that life was settled. I knew who I was, where I belonged, and where I was going. Now everything is up for grabs. All the certainties were swept away in seconds that January night. I instinctively recognised this immediately. Even as I stumbled out of the house after finding Louise's body, prominent amongst the explosion of thoughts ricocheting around my reeling brain was the realisation that nothing would ever be the same again.

But it's only now, nearly nine months later, that I am beginning to understand the full transformational impact of the events of that evening. I no longer know where I fit, who I am, or who I will be. Everything is challenged, everything is possible. It's frightening, destabilising, disorientating and full of risk – but there is also the seed of excitement and opportunity. This is the mother of all mid-life crises.

The questions tumble out in a jumbled confusion, fighting for space in my head, challenging almost everything that forms the foundation of my life. Where will I live? How shall I live? How do I honour Louise and find meaning in life, to make a difference to the world? Do I reappraise my career path in order to do so? Will I be alone or will I find another partner? Will I thrive in this new life or will I have to accept that the four-and-a-half years with Louise were as good as it ever gets?

Perhaps the most pressing question is where I will find myself living. How much longer will I be able to stay in the house that was once our home but is now just four walls and a roof? I can't continue to live here but nor can I move away. The horrific memories of the night itself, both those that are first hand (the things that I did and witnessed) and the vicarious (the re-created pictures in my mind of Louise in her final minutes) weigh me down. I need to escape, seek a fresh start where the reminders are less vivid. But this is the home that we built together. It is where I feel closest to Louise, where she is most alive. Her imprint is still visible on everything. When it is not weighing me down it comforts me. Breaking that link will be indescribably painful.

Even if I do move, where do I go? Family ties pull me in one direction, the desire to remain as close as possible to the spot where Louise's ashes are scattered drag me in another. And what type of accommodation does my new single self need? A bachelor pad or something larger in the hope of eventually finding love again? Do I accept and plan for the immediate reality of a solitary existence or try and second guess an unknown future? Somehow, having known a family home, it would be extraordinarily difficult to step down to something smaller. Downsizing in my 40's was never on the agenda.

And if I am lucky enough to find that love once more, what will it bring? While my heart clings to the hope that it would recreate what I had with Louise, my head tells me that it will inevitably be different. Indeed it must be different for the sake of all those involved, not least the new partner.

But different is unimaginable. Marriage and absorption into your partner's lifestyle and family can change who and what you are, redefining your outlook, activities and opportunities. I had settled happily and proudly into Louise's world; my social status and everything that goes with it elevated into the educated middle classes. How much of this connection will I retain? How much will be altered? There would be new places to live in and visit, new family and friends, new shared activities, a new rhythm to life, perhaps new values. Even the possibility that children will, after all, feature in my life. This chasm of uncertainty may persist for years until the 'right' person presents themselves, if they ever do. I know no more about my future than I did at 21, freshly graduated from university.

Perhaps, in some respects, I know even less than I did back then. I have found myself questioning my sense of self, direction and purpose in ways that I didn't all those years ago. This is not a drive to cleanse myself of the past but to absorb it, to fully embrace Louise within me, to honour her and ensure that, through me, she can continue to live. In the process, I am becoming a different person, both consciously and unconsciously. I do not yet know how far these changes will go and where they will take me, but I know they are happening.

And the search for meaning, the sudden desire to make a difference in Louise's name, causes me to question yet another of the cornerstones of my life which I had thought was settled upon entering the adult world; my career direction. The perspective that I have acquired during the course of Louise's illness, and subsequent events, has led me to belatedly realise that there were more worthwhile career paths I could and should have chosen 25 years ago, paths which would have allowed me, like Louise, to assist people in need every day of my working life, particularly in the field of mental health. I find myself picking up and playing with radical ideas for a complete change of direction; psychology, psychiatric nursing, counselling. Anything that can tend to that most wonderful but sometimes troubled of human features, the mind.

These are romantic indulgences. Is it realistically possible to start a new career at 47? Do I have the energy and courage to give up everything I have worked for – seniority, salary, status – in order to start again, with years of study ahead of me before I even reach the very bottom rung and find myself in a position to make that difference? My head and heart differ.

Perhaps more realistically, the question I ask myself is how can I use my recent experiences to make that difference in other ways, through charitable and voluntary work. And how can I use the power of personal narrative, of our story (my story and Louise's are two sides of the same coin) to affect the change in people's lives that would make at least some sense of Louise's death and cause her to be so pleased and proud?

This restlessness and self-examination is, like so many things on the long journey through grief, exhausting. But it is a necessary process. I cannot just revert to my former life prior to meeting Louise. She changed me too much for that. And clearly I cannot continue entirely as I was with her. So I must find a new direction.

My life has been on hold for the past nine months, during which time I have been focused entirely on survival. I don't underrate the achievement of that goal. It's the greatest of my life. But I am increasingly impatient to begin the task of moving forward since I know so painfully well how short life can be, and want to lose as little of the time left to me as possible. There is enormous sadness that this must happen without Louise but she would be the first to point out that continuing to love her does not require me to stop living. On the contrary, the greatest memorial to Louise will be to take what she gave me and made me and learn to live better still.

A Stilled Mind

23rd October | 273 days

I had a strange experience walking to my local shops the other day. I suddenly noticed that my head felt clear and light. For a moment I struggled to place the sensation, until I remembered. This is normal. Or, at least, it was before everything changed. Although the shrieking, cacophonous symphony of raw newly-minted grief began to fade some time ago, it was merely replaced with a more muted hum of deep sadness; sometimes louder, sometimes quieter, but always present. Until now. Here, for a few minutes, my mind was still, the tinnitus of grief silenced.

I've been distracted many times before now, absorbed in activities, work and discussions which briefly led me away from my new reality. But this was different. There was nothing to divert me. I was, in fact, engaged in more of the apparently never-ending bureaucracy which Louise's death has stimulated; another company requiring sight of precious documents, another trip to the Post Office to arrange for a letter to be sent by recorded delivery.

And yet I still found myself feeling… nothing in particular. And it wasn't the blank but heavy void of numbness, the state which permits us to continue to function on automatic pilot even while we struggle to comprehend the collapse of our universe. It was genuine lightness of the mind, as if I carried no burden. Not exactly happiness, but certainly not sadness either.

The respite was, of course, brief but it felt like a significant moment, a milestone on the journey. And it's consistent with a growing sense of unsteady but marked progression. Having somehow pulled myself back from the precipice of breakdown due to exhaustion a few weeks ago, I am continuing to adapt to my new reality. Day by day, almost by stealth, life without Louise is beginning to seem more normal. Deeply sad, indescribably lonely and empty, but definitely survivable.

Every month that passes, measured, of course by my new calendar which commences not on the first but the 23rd, brings a fresh sense of wonder that I have made it this far. Nine months now. We have already been apart for nearly a quarter of the time that we were married.

The world is moving on and Louise is being left behind. The recent arrival of a daughter for one of her oldest and closest friends brought me up short. Here was the first significant alteration to the landscape Louise was familiar with. At least with our niece, born two months after her death, there was the consolation that she had known of the pregnancy and even the baby's gender. But this was the first new arrival into what should have been Louise's world, about whom she knows nothing.

Not a single moment of those nine months has felt real. I still haven't remotely accepted or absorbed what happened. Sometimes I think that if I sat very still in a quiet and darkened room I would actually be able to feel the shock waves even now reverberating around my body.

But within that unreality there can still be a new normal, new routines that bring with them a form of certainty and the comfort that goes with it. My day-to-day existence has settled into a now-familiar pattern; work, networking on-line and in person with others widowed far too young, and writing and other activities to process what has happened and honour Louise's memory.

Interspersed amongst these emerging routines are increasingly set rituals designed to demonstrate, as much to myself as Louise, my continuing love for her and to acknowledge her ongoing place in my daily life. I walk the dog late at night in an empty park so that I can pray for her out loud without fear of being overheard – somehow a prayer given expression in this way feels significantly more meaningful than silent thought. I ask Louise about her day when I get in the car to return home from work, always pausing long enough to give her an opportunity to answer before telling her about mine. I kiss her pink woolly hat, still in the same place in the hallway that she left it when she returned home for the final time, whenever I enter or leave the house and on the many other occasions during the course of each day when I have a need to connect with her.

And while as a man I am denied, for both practical and cultural reasons, the type of consolation sought by the many women who wear the clothes of their lost partner, I still seek out the feel and smell of Louise by cuddling her dressing gown. My coping mechanisms are well established. I know, by this stage, what helps to get me by.

So although life remains lonely and tinged with an almost permanent melancholy, it now contains some form of structure. It's only of a temporary nature. I cannot continue to live in the same way, stuck always looking back, for the rest of my life. In time I will need to begin to overlay something else again – to grow new activities, new ways of thinking and new people around my loss so that it forms only part of me rather than the whole me.

But for the moment, at least, I know what is coming next, what to expect in the short term. That wasn't the case in the early days. This is a lost year, my life is on hold, no new worthwhile memories are being created. There is, though, a sense of stabilisation. I am still in a dark tunnel but occasional shafts of light now reach through to me and I can see that the path is becoming wider and the ceiling higher. It's less and less claustrophobic. Whereas at the beginning I could only crawl, soon I will be able stand.

Good Widower, Bad Widower

1st November | 282 days

Today, I was a good widower. Today, I drove to the spot where Louise's ashes are scattered and sat in the autumnal mist, talking to her, remembering with her, shedding tears for her, loving and honouring her.

Later, I worked on the establishment of the charity in her name and then marked All Souls Day by returning to the church which we last visited for midnight mass two years ago. I sat in the same seat that I did that far distant and special Christmas Eve and tried to focus on the words in the hymn book in front of me, as the tears swam around my eyes. I laid a flower in Louise's memory when her name was read out amongst those who have departed over the year and prayed as hard as it is possible to do. Today I did everything that a grieving widower should.

Although I reassure others on the same journey that there is no right way to grieve other than our own, that there are no rules or expectations, I am not so gentle on myself. I constantly worry about the way in which I respond to bereavement, setting my actions and emotional state against some kind of idealised notion of what I should be feeling and how I should be behaving.

I work hard to process the events of last January and honour Louise's memory. My writing, the charity, supporting Louise's family, maintaining contact with her friends, cataloguing her life, reaching out to help others who have lost. It's become my way of coping, my way of holding on to Louise. Without children to provide an alternative focus, it consumes me. I am unable to switch off. I can't settle to anything else. I don't watch TV or read. I stay up until the early hours in order to get just that little bit more done. I am utterly driven. It's a completely atypical response for somebody who normally prefers procrastination to action. But it's still not enough.

Too often, I fail to meet the standards I have set myself. Frequently it's impossible to meet them because they are contradictory. I blame myself for letting Louise down when I struggle to cope. I want to be a model for others, to be strong, to demonstrate that there is a path out of this, to find something positive which I can cling to, to reassure Louise that her solution will not be responsible for bringing me down. When I falter I loathe my weakness.

However, when I cope well, I feel guilty for being able to continue to function, as if it's a sign that I loved Louise insufficiently. I tell myself that I should be feeling worse than this. I should be prostrate, immobilised by my grief, not going to work, watching Brentford, doing the shopping in Sainsbury's. I am scornful of my resilience.

As the months go by and the shock wears off, the tears come less frequently and when they do they are quieter, more gentle, only rarely now a deeply physical all-consuming full body experience. New routines are established. Sometimes I remember how to laugh again. I may still be groggy and vulnerable, like a boxer on the ropes, but I am at least back on my feet. Yet this feeds my anxiety about the way in which I am grieving. It means that more and more frequently I find myself doing things which seem inappropriate, if only to me. When I worry that I am a bad widower.

There are days when I don't cry, when I fall asleep at night before praying for Louise, when I don't talk to her as I walk about the house, when I'm too tired to send that vital email about the charity or to go on-line to respond to people's calls for help on the forums, when I put away some small item of Louise's, when I laugh and feel normal. On these days, I tell myself that I am disrespectful. I shake myself and ask whether I have forgotten.

And I struggle with my physical desires. These didn't die with Louise and when I satisfy them in the only way that I now can, I try hard not to fantasise about her because it would seem wrong to do so about somebody who is dead. But it's even more inconceivable and inappropriate to fantasise about somebody else. There is no right, only wrong, and a sense of disloyalty. This is magnified when I have, on occasion, found myself reluctantly admiring another woman. Louise wanted me to find love again but I scold myself for the knowledge that I will be open to the prospect sooner rather than later.

I often ask myself how Louise would be coping if the situation were reversed, convinced that she would somehow be handling things much better even though the reality would, I suspect, be more nuanced. Our differing strengths and personalities mean each of us would have found some aspects of grief and widowhood harder to deal with than others.

This sense that Louise is watching, judging, measuring the extent of my love, the quality of our relationship and my worthiness as a husband is, I know, ridiculous. Even if it is possible for her to do so, nothing would be less likely. Louise was the least judgemental person I know. She would accept that I am doing my best, understand the limitations on my capacity, and ask for no more. She would understand that her illness and death was about her but beyond that point this experience, the journey through bereavement, is owned by me. I must make my own rules.

And therein lies the problem. The lack of rules. Modern western liberal society with its emphasis on the primacy of the individual largely allows us the freedom to make our own way through the experience of loss. There are relatively few societal guidelines and norms, the Victorian notion of structured mourning long since discarded and derided. Sometimes though, a light shining through the fog of confusion to guide us along the way would be welcomed. When it is difficult to think for yourself, or you do not know what to think, conformity is both easy and reassuring.

In the absence of any clear cultural sense of direction I have to make do with my own, very personal compass, my own sense of what is right, or rather, what is right for me. The test is at once both apparently simple and immensely challenging. In order to be a 'good' widower, to come through this feeling that I've navigated the journey well, I have to make Louise proud of me.

This should be straightforward. Louise will understand that life is messy, tiring and complicated. An idealised form of beautifully pure mourning could not fully survive contact with it. The resulting compromises, confusion, mistakes, guilt and omissions do not mean that I love her any the less. Nor do they make me, retrospectively, a bad or uncaring husband or, now, a bad and uncaring widower. I know that Louise is cheering me on, always my biggest fan, whether I deserved it or not. I know that I am doing all I can to honour her in the way that she deserves. I know that she is proud of me.

But somehow I am still confronted with the same dilemma; how can I possibly ever do enough to properly capture and celebrate a life so beautiful, so full, so generous, so full of fun and achievement and one that profoundly touched so many? It's an impossible task. No matter how hard I try, my words, deeds and thoughts can never be remotely sufficient to do justice to Louise, to keep her essence alive. As a consequence, I feel as though I have failed her. But it doesn't mean that I am a bad widower. Rather, it means that I am incredibly blessed to have been the husband of such a remarkable woman.

Maintaining Standards

When we moved into our current home, the one luxury purchase that we allowed ourselves was a large and ever-so-slightly stylish dining room table. This was the house we were going to live in for the rest of our lives and we envisaged many years of entertaining large gatherings of family and friends. The rooms would be full of people we loved and admired and the walls would ring to the sound of their conversation and laughter. Now, even while the hopes and ambition mock me, that same dining room table is something of a symbol of my determination not to collapse into chaos.

Louise's death has led to a swift recalibration of my sense of achievement. When the heart and soul is ripped out of our existence, one of the first things that is threatened is the veneer of order and routine that normally sustains us, nourishes our self-identity.

Like a ship which has broken free of its moorings – stability, direction, and control are lost. There is nothing to anchor us. Motivation evaporates. Purpose is destroyed. The chore of daily living becomes overwhelming. Easy everyday tasks become difficult. Difficult tasks become impossible. Essential tasks become optional. In these circumstances, the real measure of success becomes not those by which we normally judge ourselves, perhaps academic achievement or career progression, but getting out of bed – or at least getting out of bed on a morning.

Some people are temperamentally well-placed to deal with this, if only in the early days of bereavement, before exhaustion overwhelms them. They instinctively respond to crisis with frantic displacement activity, a need to clean, cook, wash, do anything which can mask or dislodge the pain. Louise was one of those people. I am not. My default reaction to fear, anxiety or distress is to become paralysed with listlessness.

Even in the distant good times, I muddled through life with a slight air of disorganisation. Louise provided my structure and momentum. She was practical, organised, purposeful. Whereas I talked about doing things, she did them. Adrift without her, and floored by grief, there was a very real danger that I would sink into a mire of apathetic helplessness.

And it's true that there have been some things I'm not proud of. Not going to bed in the middle of the night because I hadn't the energy to get off the sofa.

Getting up in the middle of the day because I hadn't the energy to get out of bed in the morning. Arriving at work late almost every day for the first six months. Reaching the point where most of the lights in the house were out because it was just too difficult to establish which bulbs I needed to buy and then go and purchase them. Abandoning my daily ritual of a hot shower because it took too much effort and… well, what was the point? Nobody was cuddling me. Nobody was sharing my space. Nobody was sharing my bed.

But while it's been a constant struggle, I'm still afloat. The house is still orderly, the garden, although slightly ragged around the edges, is still broadly respectable, my clothes are still clean, there is still food in the cupboards. I admit I cheat. I am grateful that I can afford to employ somebody to clean the house once a fortnight. My first independent purchase was a new dishwasher. I swallow the hefty daily parking charges and drive into work rather than waste precious sleeping time by getting up early enough to take the bus. But I'm gentle enough on myself to allow these shortcuts.

And every evening, I still sit down to eat at that large dining room table. It's a desperately lonely experience. Other than climbing into an empty bed, almost nothing reinforces Louise's absence more. We almost always ate dinner together no matter how late one or other, or both of us, got home from work. It was the time we talked about the day, discussed stories in the news, planned our futures. And we did so amidst a clutter of Louise's possessions. She used the table as an informal workstation and it was usually occupied with her laptop, sketchbooks and piles of course notes and BMJs. Now these signs of her existence are gone and I sit eating in isolation, alone save for my iPad.

Yet every time that I do so is a triumph of sorts, a gesture of defiance from which I draw strength and pride. I am not taking the easy option and eating from my lap in front of the TV. I may struggle in other ways but here, and with countless similar small gestures, at least I'm maintaining some standards and self-discipline. It's a token of order, normality and continuity. A sign of my determination to survive. I may be lethargic, forgetful and disorganised but I am still holding on to my sanity and self-respect. Chaos is staved off for another day.

Surviving Suicide

9th November | 290 days

How do you come to terms with the suicide of your partner? How do you deal not just with the shock of the sudden loss of the person who you loved more than any other, who shaped and defined your life more than any other, but also with the knowledge that they died voluntarily? How do you cope with the fact that it needn't have happened, with the sheer pointless waste, and with the violence inherent both in the act itself and the force of its consequences? And how do you manage the thought that your loved one chose to leave you, and in the process put you through your own hell, to wreck your life as well as theirs?

Suicide is different to other forms of bereavement. That is not to say that other forms of loss are somehow easier to bear because, self-evidently, that isn't the case. Regardless of the cause, the death of a partner has the capacity to crush those left behind, to provoke a quite extraordinary intensity and range of emotional response. Overlaid on the pain, despair and loneliness there is almost always confusion, guilt, fear and bewilderment.

But suicide also brings with it a very particular set of additional burdens. Not just heightened guilt and anger but also betrayal, rejection and, sometimes still, stigma. There is something about a person ending their own life, something so inexplicable, wasteful and dark, that it stirs a deep, horrified, visceral response in us all. Even within the young widowed community itself, many of my peers, hardened by bitter experience to most tales of tragedy and loss, find it difficult to know how to respond when they learn of Louise's story.

And even now, in today's apparently enlightened society, many who have lost in this way cannot bring themselves to openly acknowledge the real cause of death for fear of the critical and judgemental reaction of family and friends, a reaction that would be unthinkable where the cause of death is cancer or heart disease. I know, for I have been told, that behind my back I am the subject of cruel and unfounded rumour and idle gossip amongst my neighbours as they ignorantly speculate on what 'really' caused Louise to take her life. I have even received hate mail accusing me of responsibility. Suicide is a death, and a loss, like no other.

The unique impact of suicide on those left behind is recognised in the existence of the term 'suicide survivor', used to indicate somebody affected by this form of death. In few other circumstances are the widowed so clearly defined not only by their loss but also by the cause of that loss.

Those who have experienced the death of their loved one in this manner are twice as likely to suffer from complicated grief, the condition of prolonged acute raw grieving, than those bereaved by other means. They are also at significantly greater risk of suffering Post Traumatic Stress Disorder and depression than those bereaved in almost any other way. And in perhaps the greatest and most tragic of ironies they are also particularly vulnerable to suicide themselves.

So I ask myself how have I managed to regain my equilibrium relatively quickly? How do I manage to continue to live in the same house? How am I able to be sit here writing this just a few feet from the spot where I found Louise, able to glance across and see it right now, and to pass and re-pass it dozens of times every day, and yet to do so calmly despite always remembering? How can the image of Louise, her face battleship grey, eyes open but unseeing, be seared into my memory yet I barely respond to it? How can I interact with my colleagues at work as though nothing untoward has happened? Why have there been relatively few nightmares and no flashbacks, no obvious symptoms of complicated grief or PTSD?

Sometimes, this is a source of shame. I tell myself that I should be feeling this more, that coping so well is disrespectful to Louise. On other occasions I find myself almost exhilarated, proud of the fact that I *am* coping. If I can do this, I can do anything. I am invincible.

Except, of course, I'm not. The powers of resilience we are blessed with never cease to amaze me but there have been clear signs of physical and mental stress. Waves of exhaustion threaten to overwhelm me every few weeks. It's only within the last couple of months that the night sweats have stopped and my pillow is no longer drenched in perspiration when I wake on a morning. I convinced myself that I was dying after suffering for several weeks with a persistent and distressing lump in my throat, now diagnosed, after hospital investigations, as a hysterical reaction. And the sense of detachment from the images in my mind that protects me so effectively from the impact of them is itself a form of psychological strain and disorder. The life that I have found myself living is simply so unreal that I do not, cannot, associate it with mine. I have parted company with my own reality.

I am a suicide survivor and marked as such. I carry the burden of guilt almost universally held by those in my circumstances. The guilt that I could not, did not, do more to prevent Louise from acting upon her intentions. Not a day goes by day without me replaying in my mind the events of that evening, constructing elaborate alternative scenarios, in all of which I save Louise. The adrenaline surges as I imagine reaching her in time. As the story unfolds, so something like hope emerges only to be cruelly crushed when I reluctantly prise myself away from the comforting fiction and return to my new unreal reality.

And I return a failure. The man who was supposed to be his wife's rock, the man whom she was supposed to be able to trust to guide her through her darkest days, but I couldn't even perform the most basic of functions, that of keeping her alive.

And I now live in a world where I have come to expect the very worst. As a consequence I'm on edge, ready to see and exaggerate danger. This was powerfully brought home to me by my disproportionate reaction when my Mother-in-Law unexpectedly failed to answer her front door or respond to phone calls when I dropped by on the first anniversary of the day that Louise's father had taken his life. I panicked, seeing only one possible reason and assumed this was a mirror image of the events I have already endured twice over. It eventually transpired that there was, of course, a perfectly innocent explanation. All was well. But it was telling that this surprised me almost as much as it relieved me.

Nevertheless the label 'suicide survivor' need not just denote mere victimhood. Survival, in these circumstances, is achievement in itself and requires an accommodation, conscious or otherwise, with the pressures and emotions engendered by this unique form of loss. Suicide will not allow itself to be ignored. It will not go away. It must be acknowledged and understood. Some form of compromise with it must be reached in order to be able to emerge from the half-life led in its shadow.

I'm more fortunate in this respect than some. There is no sense of mystery, no need to search for answers or cast around for countless reasons to blame myself for the causes of Louise's death. Unlike many for whom there are no warning signs, I know what was in Louise's mind and why. Her state of mind, her depression and anxiety were constant topics of discussion during our time together. I knew in those final weeks that thoughts of suicide had entered her head, even if she hid the intensity of them from me and sought to reassure me that there was no risk. Had I still been in any doubt, her farewell letter to me was detailed and eloquent. I understand.

This, in turn, helps me to place boundaries around my guilt, boundaries that contain it, prevent it from overwhelming me. It may be that I should have been able to protect Louise from the consequences of her illness but at least I am clear that I wasn't responsible for it. Or, at least, I am on good days.

And entirely unconsciously I have managed to arrive at a particular settled narrative of the events surrounding Louise's death which brings some form of peace and acceptance, an interpretation which I can come to terms with. By choosing from the very first to concentrate on Louise's illness and the selflessness of her actions, I have written a history that I can cope with, that meets my emotional needs. It was not an act of free will. It was imbued with love and concern for me and the rest of the family. There is thus no cause for anger or a sense of rejection. I tell myself that Louise left me precisely because she loved me, not because she didn't. I genuinely believe this to be the truth, but even if it isn't, it doesn't matter, because it's my truth.

I have also found a way to deal with the senselessness of Louise's loss. I find it hard to accept the trite and commonplace consolations so often offered; that everything happens for a reason, that there are always positives to be drawn, that this was, somehow, part of God's grander scheme. The world would be a better, kinder, gentler place, and my life would be infinitely richer and happier had Louise managed to resist her compulsion on that January afternoon.

But they do nevertheless speak to a real need. I must be able to hold on to *something*. I need to know that the light Louise shone on the world has not been completely extinguished, that the fact and manner of her death brings about some kind of change for the better. So I have found a purpose in helping others, reaching out through support networks and my writing to engage those who find themselves in a similar situation to me, attempting, so far as I can, to educate others about mental illness and establishing a charity in Louise's name to assist other medical practitioners in crisis.

None of this activity even begins to even up the balance sheet but it provides me with a degree of fulfilment and makes some kind of sense of events. The very worst having happened, I can at least feel that Louise would approve of my response to it.

Louise's suicide presents me with a choice, a choice either to shrink or grow. But if I was to choose the former I would essentially be doing what her illness caused Louise to do; give up on life. I cannot think of anything which would cause her more distress and upset than the thought that she had been responsible for that. I may be grieving but I do not have the excuse of mental illness.

For Louise's sake I therefore have a responsibility to attempt to rise to the challenge, to enlarge my life, to live it as positively and well as possible and to help others along the way. The experience of suicide will always be part of me but it will not beat me, and if it shapes me then I am determined that it will be for the better.

Waiting for Signs

14th November | 295 days

I had resisted the temptation for months until, finally, I cracked. Sitting under the trees around which Louise's ashes were scattered, in a moment of desperation I choked back the tears for long enough to ask her for a sign, an indication that she was in heaven and that she was happy.

One of the privileges of this journey through grief (and they do exist even if you have to look very hard to find them) is that it has enabled me to finally understand what pure love is, and to know that I have been blessed to experience it. The highest form of love isn't really about desire, longing, attraction, passion, compassion, understanding or a need for physical contact and intimacy, though all of those things feature in it.

I have discovered, that it is, rather, essentially about an intrinsic unselfishness, an intense desire for the happiness and wellbeing of another person to the point where you place their interests and needs above your own. Had I been a parent I might have come to this realisation earlier. But now Louise has enabled me to know. I find myself caring more about what is happening to her, what she is now experiencing, than I do my own immediate needs.

I tell myself over and over that separation from Louise, her absence from my life, would be tolerable provided that I know that she still exists in some meaningful and recognisable form and is happy. If Louise is happy then so shall I be. The not knowing, however, is unbearable. She has disappeared into a complete void. Nobody can provide me with the reassurance I crave other than Louise herself.

Others in my position report signs, events, or experiences that confirm in their own mind the continuing presence and happiness of their partner. Putting aside rationality and scepticism in my emotional vulnerability, I yearn for the comfort that this must bring. But however hard I have looked I have found nothing myself. Not so much as a single coincidence that I could hold on to. A particularly vivid dream in the early days, one in which Louise was leaning over me as I lay in bed and was so lifelike that for the briefest of moments – a split second – I experienced the most remarkable inner glow of peace and happiness was dismissed as just that: a vivid dream.

To my astonishment I briefly found myself contemplating an attempt to make contact with Louise via a spiritualist. As somebody who in addition to those aspirations to high-minded rationalism still also holds a primitive fear of the consequences of calling up unknown worlds, it was·the last place that I expected to find myself in. But I should know by now that this journey leads us to unlikely destinations and I was eventually only dissuaded by the knowledge of Louise's probable disappointment with me for thinking in such terms.

Or rather, that was one of the reasons. The other, equally compelling, was a fear of asking in case it brought no response. What would that mean then? The risk was every bit as great as the potential reward.

So I was careful not to ask for anything until that moment under Louise's trees when I weakened. In the days and weeks that followed I waited anxiously for some extraordinary coincidence or inexplicable event to answer my cry for acknowledgement and reassurance. I didn't know what I was looking for but felt sure that I would recognise it as soon as I saw it.

Nothing.

Not a single thing turned up that I could hold on to. Since I cannot believe that Louise would not answer me, seek to comfort me, if she possibly could, and for the sake of my sanity I cannot allow myself to believe that she does not do so because she no longer exists in any form, I now need to rationalise this disappointment.

Perhaps Louise *has* previously reached out to me and I have missed the significance – was I meant to find meaning in that battered old family hand-me-down nursing manual which mysteriously fell off the bookcase? But then why should she speak to me so opaquely? Why does it seem that such messages only ever come wrapped in riddles? Maybe, knowing my nervousness of ghosts and the spirit world, Louise has decided not to frighten me, not to give me any more cause to be anxious in my own home.

Or perhaps, as her Christian friends and family hold, Louise has simply moved on to a higher plane and genuinely found peace with God in a place where she can no longer connect with this world. If that is the right place for her to be then I am genuinely happy for her, even if the thought simultaneously makes me feel even more lost and alone for myself.

None of these explanations entirely convince me but any or all of them are sufficiently plausible to serve to continue to allow me to hope; for Louise's continuing being, for her happiness, and for the possibility of us one day being reunited. I will not get closer to a definitive answer so, in this life at least, they will have to suffice. Louise continues to speak to me, even in the silence.

Receiving Signs

20th November | 301 days

Perhaps Louise is closer to me than I dared hope. Barely a week after writing about the lack of signs, I left the house this morning to discover a small white feather sitting nestled between her muddy walking boots which still sit in our outer porch.

Rationally, I know that this must simply be a coincidence. Before Louise died I would have been dismissive of anybody seeking to find meaning in such a simple occurrence. How many countless times over the years must I have come across white feathers without ascribing any significance to them, without even noticing them? I'm emotional, vulnerable, and actively searching for meaning everywhere that I look. In these circumstances, I am almost bound to find something but the value of what I find deserves to be questioned even more closely than would otherwise be the case. I know the risk of confirmation bias.

Yet I can't help myself from setting aside the scepticism. In spiritual terms, white feathers are seen by some as signifying the presence of a recently departed loved one, a token of protection and love sent by a guardian angel. The porch is partly protected from the elements. It's not somewhere you might expect a feather to drift, particularly when there are no others in the vicinity. The likelihood of a random feather coming to rest on Louise's boots, sitting proud on top as if it was being offered up directly by her, must be infinitesimally small.

And it reminds me that I came across another single white feather in the back garden some time ago. I largely disregarded it because the coincidences and the symbolism did not seem as strong but brought it inside for safekeeping nevertheless. Somehow a feather seems the most appropriate of all ways in which Louise might choose to communicate with me given her fascination with the small and everyday beauties of the natural world around us. Both feathers now sit on a shelf alongside her fading collection of pine cones, conkers, and assorted flora.

I am almost embarrassed to find myself writing in these terms. Guardian angels? I can imagine Louise's gentle but firm dismissal of the concept. And why now and not before, when I was still reverberating with shock and the raw intensity of the pain of loss was shredding my soul?

But I still need something to hold on to. I deserve to allow myself comfort and hope from whatever source I can find them. The thought that this might be a sign that Louise is close by, with me, watching me, communicating with me, makes me happier than anything else during these ten long months, even if – at the same time – it concerns me that I might be inadvertently holding her back from wherever she might need to be.

It may well be almost a conscious self-deceit but there can be no harm, and much good, in me choosing to interpret this as evidence that Louise is still by my side. I am trying to move beyond grief and mourning, to lift my head and look towards recovery, focusing on the life that I must re-make. The belief that Louise is with me, and that we might therefore one day be re-united in some form, will enable me to do so with all the more strength and confidence. I suddenly feel less alone.

Ten Minutes More

23rd November | 304 days

On that Friday morning I slept in late, exhausted by the strain of the previous weeks and months. I was half woken by Louise gently squeezing my toes as she walked past the bottom of the bed. She announced that she was about to leave and just as had happened a thousand times before she kissed me tenderly, told me that she loved me and wished me a good day. I groggily responded in the same terms. I can't recall if I was sufficiently awake even to open my eyes to look at her.

A few minutes later, as I struggled into the bathroom, I heard the front door close. I thought that it was odd that Louise hadn't come upstairs one more time to say a final goodbye now that I was awake, or that she didn't at least call out. It seemed unusually distant.

We had spoken to each other for the last time.

Sudden death changes worlds in seconds. The moment when I returned home later that evening and saw the lights on in an unusual pattern and a note on the front door, even before I was close enough to read the note, I knew. Everything that I valued about my life, everything that I thought was certain about my future, was ripped away from me. In that instant, without warning, I lost love, companionship, emotional support, physical intimacy, friendship circles, status, financial certainty and my sense of self. There was no time to prepare, no time to say goodbye. Louise was here and then she wasn't. My world was normal and then it wasn't.

I struggle to comprehend how Louise could have so calmly said goodbye to me that morning in the knowledge that it was for the last time. How could she have faced me, even wished me a good day, knowing what she was about to inflict on both of us?

It's possible that she didn't know for certain. Her farewell letter had been written a couple of days before but emails and notes she scribbled during the day speak of somebody who was preparing to live as well as to die. It seems clear from the evidence that I have managed to piece together that she aborted plans for an even more violent attempt on her life during the course of the day before returning home. It remains a consolation. She was fighting the compulsion as hard as she knew how right up to the last minute. Nevertheless, on at least one level she was aware, when she woke me, that she was about to walk out of my life – and hers.

Ten months later, I haven't let Louise go. I still talk to her every day. I tell her about my day and ask about hers. I ask for her opinion and advice. I reminisce about our shared moments. I read out loud to her the postcards, letters and emails from family and friends. I will read this out to her, just as I do everything that I write. Sometimes, I instinctively check myself before saying something which might have made her anxious, still self-censoring even though she is now a long way beyond hurt and pain.

But I'm talking into a void. My questions aren't met with a response. When I tell her that I love her, when I apologise for letting her down in those final days, I don't know if she hears me.

I long to be able to say goodbye properly. There is so much that I need to say, so much that I didn't say, or didn't say often enough, in the course of daily life. I wish with all my heart that I could have just ten minutes more with her. It doesn't seem much to ask for, on top of four-and-a-half years. Ten minutes, in which I would remember all over again what it felt like to be with Louise, to hungrily absorb the sight of her, her voice, her eyes, the warmth of her body, to hug, kiss and hold her once more. I would concentrate so hard to imprint it all on my consciousness so that I would faithfully retain every detail for a lifetime.

But, most of all, I want that ten minutes so that I could tell Louise everything that I need in order to be at peace, everything that I would have said had I known what was to come, enough for me to be sure that when we parted she would carry with her the comfort of knowing everything. I would tell her how much I love her and why. I would tell her how intensely proud I am of her and how remarkable she is. I would tell her how desperately sorry I am for letting her down and I would tell her how I understand.

I remember now that prior to her last Christmas she asked whether I could do another '50 reasons why I love you' letter, of the type that I had written to her early in our relationship. I fully intended to do it but it became lost in the daily struggle to keep things going at that time, to support Louise through her crisis, to support my Mother through her own very serious illness, the complications in family relations which were a consequence of these pressures, and to manage my busy job. I was exhausted and half forgot the request. When I remembered, it never seemed to be the right time to sit down and do it. In truth, not understanding exactly where Louise's mind was taking her by this time, I was also slightly put out that such a thing should be written to order when its real value surely came from its spontaneity.

But with hindsight, now knowing the struggle in Louise's mind at that time, it's clear that she was asking not for narcissistic reasons but because she was desperate, because she needed something to hold on to, reasons to believe that she deserved to live. I failed her.

Although we declared our love for each other several times every day, in person and by text, I therefore need to go further than this, to tell her how much I really love her. I need to tell her how she made my heart sing, how every day I shook my head in disbelief at my good fortune in finding her. I need to tell her that she provided me with everything that I had ever dared hope for and much more besides. I need to tell her that my love is unconditional and total, that I never expected to feel so strongly for another person, nor even knew that it was possible. I need to tell her of the 200 reasons why I love her that I have now listed.

I also worry that I didn't properly explain to Louise how her pride in me was reciprocated. I could never quite work out why she spoke about me so proudly. I didn't do anything very remarkable but she habitually referred to me as 'my wonderful husband'. I drank this all in like the purest nectar. For somebody as special as Louise to be proud of me was the greatest, most empowering feeling I have ever experienced. I almost miss her pride in me even more than her love.

But I don't think that I ever truly sat down and told her exactly how my heart swelled so much that it was fit to burst whenever I thought of her. I think it was so self-evident to me, so much part of the natural order of things, that it didn't really occur to me that it might need to be said. I tended to forget that she didn't hear me when I was driving my friends and work colleagues to distraction by my constant chatter about my amazing wife. She didn't hear me drop her proudly into every conversation I possibly could, whether it be with the barber, the GP, or the call centre employee.

And she herself certainly never saw what I could so clearly. She never understood how highly regarded she was professionally, admired by her colleagues and loved by her patients. She was oblivious to her exceptional intelligence and intuitive wisdom, the rigour of her restlessly enquiring mind, the remarkable nature of her empathy and love for others, her ability to see the beauty in everybody and everything, the lovely in the unlovely. She discounted her creative and artistic skills and downplayed her athletic achievements. She never realised exactly how much of a difference her vibrant energy, happiness, and love of life brought to others.

Nor did Louise appreciate how extraordinary her gentle nature was, quite how unusual it is to be entirely without the vice of anger. She didn't recognise her bravery and resilience in fighting her illness. She would be astonished to know that she was the very embodiment of the state of grace which was spiritually so significant for her. She didn't know, and I didn't tell her. Or at least, I didn't tell her frequently enough.

I now wonder how much Louise might have been fortified by me declaring both my love for her and my pride in her even more loudly and clearly, whether it would have been enough to help combat some of the self-doubt and perhaps give her sufficient strength to have held on when the darkness submerged her.

This is why I also need to tell Louise how sorry I am. And not just for these omissions but for failing her so badly when she needed me most, for failing to spot the signs, or at least grossly underestimating the level of risk, and for making the wrong calls, even if they were with all the right intentions.

Ten minutes is very little time for me to say all this, but then I would not need Louise to speak at all, other than to let me hear her voice. She has nothing to explain to me, nothing that she needs to justify or apologise for. I want her to know that I am certain of her love, that I understand why she was driven to do what she did, that I do not blame her and that I am not angry with her.

I could, and should, have said these things during the course of our years together. Over and over again. I regret with all my heart that I cannot have those ten minutes in order to put that right but console myself with the hope that I will one day have all eternity to do so.

Pushing the Boundaries

1st December | 312 days

Take a deep breath and keep on walking. Focus on the far side of the bridge. Don't glance at the spot where we had our photo taken after one of our first visits to the theatre together and where others are now posing for the camera. Don't think about the Whitehall Gardens immediately behind me, where we decided to give things another try after a short break up in the early days. Try not to look at the glittering night time panorama of London, sweeping across the Thames and taking in St Paul's Cathedral, the distant behemoths of the Square Mile and across to the Shard, the Oxo Tower and the South Bank. Our skyline. Our city. Ignore the couples walking hand in hand, huddling together against the cold. Hand the beggar a pound because Louise would always do so. Choke back the welling tears and make it across.

Although born in South Africa and raised in Surrey, Louise was a London girl to the core. Until we returned from our Whitechapel flat to the suburbs, we lived our version of the metropolitan middle class lifestyle, spoilt by the easy access to a vast array of shows, exhibitions, museums, parks and restaurants. We hungrily absorbed the artistic, cultural, political and historical highlights. We may not always have understood them but we were keen to challenge ourselves. London was our playground and the South Bank our favourite corner of it.

Which was why returning to the very heart of that life for the first time since Louise's death was enough to threaten my first breakdown in public for several months. The award-winning Hungerford Footbridges which connect the Victoria Embankment and the South Bank are the busiest in London: modern steel and concrete structures crossed by 8.5 million pedestrians each year.

Yet my passage felt as lonely, precarious and as challenging as a high wire walk across a deep gorge. This was a bridge that we crossed and re-crossed together so many times. We never failed to stop to admire the view. It seems like no time at all since I was walking across it on my way home after our second date, light-headed, with disbelieving happiness at the good fortune which had suddenly engulfed me. Then I had gained more than I had ever dared dream of. Now I have lost it. A full circle of life.

Always sentimental, always vulnerable to the emotional significance of place, I feel Louise's loss particularly keenly in those locations which played a part, however fleeting, however mundane, in our lives together. Towns we visited, restaurants we ate in, museums we attended, train stations we stopped at, supermarkets we shopped in, roads we walked down. Every single one of them carries a memory. My mind wanders back to the moments we shared there, airbrushing out today's crowds and traffic and superimposing a ghostly vision of us, as we were then. The streets, buildings and landscapes are the same so it's a struggle to understand how Louise too is not still here.

I mentally divide locations into two categories, those which are 'safe' because they played no part in our lives together, and the rest, all of which are approached with trepidation, as if crossing an emotional minefield. Certain places, those close to home, are impossible to avoid and I have become hardened to them as the months go by. The second visit easier than the first, the third better again. Gradually, by repetition, they lose their sting.

But substantial areas have remained off limits. Places that are simply too emotionally difficult to return to. Some are easier to avoid than others. I'm unlikely, on a day-to-day basis, to have cause to visit the deserted romantic beaches of the Northumberland coast or Kardamyli, the Peloponnesian village nestled between the Taygetos Mountains and the Messenian Bay which we thought we would return to again and again. But London, a city of 8 million people on our doorstep, is impossible to ignore.

Bit by bit, I have been cautiously renewing acquaintance with the capital in recent months, conscious that I cannot allow myself to be a prisoner of those memories for ever. Rather than decline opportunities, as I did during the early days, I have more recently been determined to accept the challenge and go wherever invitations and events take me. Therapy by Oyster card.

So I have once again wandered the streets of central London on my way to restaurants, pubs, meetings and conferences, extending my boundaries as I go. I have sat on the low retaining wall outside City Hall where we shared our first kiss, found myself on Louise's daily route to her Bermondsey Practice, ventured onto the District and Central lines through our former home stations, and stood still amongst the movement of busy commuter crowds, staring transfixed at the car park of a wine merchants near Liverpool Street Station, lost in the moment four years previously when we were returning glasses from our wedding reception.

Louise's absence has been felt at every step. How can I be in these places without her being by my side? I push my hands deeper into my pockets, trying to fight the instinctive urge to hold one of them out ready to find hers. Completely lacking in any natural sense of direction myself, I stumble around uncertainly, yearning to be able once more to relax and follow Louise, with her intimate knowledge of every side street and shortcut. And I hope no passers-by hear as I talk to her under my breath at every point of resonance, trying still to share our memories. 'Do you remember when we...?'

Some particularly cherished places still remain beyond reach. The immediate environs of our old flat, the Bethnal Green church we married in, Victoria Park, in which we shared so many walks and cycle rides as well as the excitement of the Olympic Games on our doorstep... and, until now, the section of the South Bank that was dearest to Louise, the cultural hub around the South Bank Centre, a place which spoke to her love of performance, curiosity and learning. A place accessed via the Hungerford footbridge.

I had no need to take that route across the bridge. I could have avoided it and kept the memories locked away. But memories that I cannot trust myself with are no memory at all. If they are all I have left then I have to learn how to safely set them free and, in time, draw comfort and pleasure from them. I cannot allow myself to be limited either emotionally or practically by the boundaries they impose.

A short walk across a footbridge, painful though it was, therefore represented another significant landmark in my journey towards a new life, helping me towards reclaiming both a special place and a host of precious memories.

Committing an Offence

10th December | 321 days

Ten months after Louise's death, the cause of it has finally been formally recognised. What was obvious to me even before I had managed to break into the house to find her body is now a matter of public record; Louise took her life. I will, at last, receive a death certificate.

The journey to this point has been tortuous. While the need to establish beyond doubt the cause of death from unnatural causes is clear, the inquest process in England and Wales is not designed to take account of the needs of the bereaved family. Time and time again, the impression was created that I was an inconvenience, held almost in a certain casual contempt by a local Coroner's office mired in controversy and allegations of malpractice and overwhelmed by an almost complete breakdown of service.

Indignity was piled upon indignity, from the hours spent waiting in a call queuing system on the phone in the days after Louise's death simply to try to find out whether her body would be released in time for the funeral, to the inquest dates cancelled without notification and the lazy interim notice of death so strewn with typographical errors that Louise's identity was mangled almost beyond recognition.

But worse than this, worse than the procedural errors and delays on the day of the inquest itself, and worse even than standing in a witness box in a public court to be cross-examined about the private anguish and mental state of my beloved wife in her final days, was the delivery of the coroner's verdict. Louise, he declared, had 'committed suicide'.

It was not the inevitable verdict that upset me but the careless language. Suicide was decriminalised in England in 1961. We pride ourselves on living in a more enlightened age, one which understands and recognises the dark force of mental illness and accords those driven to take their lives under its malign influence the same care and respect as those who have died by any other means. But the language from that brutal legal framework, one which reflected the societal prejudices of its day, is still with us.

The phrase 'committed suicide' is so pervasive, so commonplace, that I can hardly blame the coroner himself for using it. We fall back on it instinctively. In a game of word association, the two words would be inextricably linked. If you are not directly affected by the act of suicide you would have no reason to reflect upon its usage, much less challenge it.

But if you are, then the term jumps out at you and hits you squarely between the eyes, knocking you for six with its entirely inappropriate connotations of blame and criminality. Nobody would think that it's acceptable to say that somebody has committed death by cancer or heart disease so why should we persist in doing so with suicide? Alternatives exist. 'Died by suicide' might sound a clumsy and unnatural formulation but only because it is so rarely heard.

No doubt some would argue that they're only words. But language does not exist in a vacuum. They are words which unthinkingly betray a lack of respect and consideration for the victims of this particular form of disease, and for their relatives. They suggest that for all the lip service paid to mental illness there remains remnants of the dismissive and hostile attitudes more openly held towards it generations ago.

And those residual prejudices continue to be reflected in choices in healthcare funding where mental health services persistently find themselves relatively less well-resourced than other branches of medicine. Somewhere along the line, words – and the attitudes they consciously or unconsciously represent – form part of a chain of cultural ignorance which ends in real suffering and real death.

The implication that those driven by darkness and desperation to such extreme and tragic measures are somehow guilty of wrongdoing says more about the society which tolerates such attitudes than it does about those who it persists in misunderstanding and maligning. Perhaps we haven't progressed as far during the course of the past 50 years as we would like to think.

Making New Memories

12th December | 323 days

I bought a mug last weekend. An unremarkable, cheap souvenir of a short continental city break. The kind that can be found in kitchens all over the country. But this particular mug represents something profound, something of incalculable value, something so unexpected that it has almost floored me. It symbolises the creation of new memories and in doing so marks the first genuine proof that this new life can still be worth living.

It wasn't just Louise's life which stopped on that January evening. Although mine was not ended, it has effectively been on hold ever since. As each successive day has given way to another and the rawest of grief, the acute pain, has gradually subsided, I have stumbled my way through ten months on automatic pilot, seeing, doing, but rarely feeling.

Anaesthetised by shock, I have survived but achieved nothing else. Whereas, before, life was rich with a succession of moments which I savoured and hoped to be able to remember for ever, no new memories have been created in the course of the last 10 months. Nothing has happened which interests or excites me, nothing which I will ever wish to remember. The year has been a void, offering nothing more than the daily grind of getting by. Stabilisation, it seemed, was all I could realistically hope for at present.

But out of nowhere this monochrome life has suddenly been splashed with colour. A weekend in Bruges with nearly 30 of my new friends in the community of young widowers has transformed my horizons, serving to remind me that life retains the capacity to be good. Not right, and certainly not better than it was before. But still good, and that is revelatory.

I have been uplifted by spending three days in the company of resilient, wise, compassionate, inspirational and brave people, all of whom have known tragedy, all of whom have a heart-breaking story to tell, but all of whom have chosen to fight for a new life over surrender to the loss of the old. It was good-humoured, supportive, sometimes reflective, sometimes raucous and, ultimately, immensely hopeful. Almost every one of us was re-learning how to enjoy ourselves, testing and revelling in our ability to do so within the context of a safe community and the certainty of mutual understanding. Within this bubble, surrounded by others in a similar position, we were normal again.

It's true that there were tears and conversations of the type that would have made those listening in on adjacent tables recoil with horror (close familiarity with death leads to a certain casual attitude towards the detail of it which can be shocking to those removed from the experience). But the weekend was also filled with the normal tourist activities: overeating, drinking, shopping and sightseeing.

And most of all, there was laughter. Much of the humour was as black as coal, directed at our own fate. Mocking bereavement, particularly when there is safety in numbers, allows us all to feel a little braver. But there was also the banter and good-humoured teasing to be found in any large high-spirited group. I laughed more in three days than I have in the past ten months. And it was not the shallow mechanical laughter which has been the best I could manage up to now, but deep, genuine and instinctive. I had forgotten what it felt like to experience pleasure and fun. And now I did so not just for a few moments, or even hours, but sustained over an entire long weekend.

Even better, I was able to display that happiness without fear of giving the wrong impression about the extent of my recovery. I had no need to worry that my smiles and laughter might be misinterpreted. Here, everybody understood that a good weekend did not mean that I no longer loved Louise, no longer missed her or no longer mourned her. It did not mean that I was back to normal, that somehow things were now all right again. Here it was understood that it simply meant I was enjoying some respite. It was not a cure but a release.

I still felt Louise's absence, of course, but my time was so full and the company so good that it no longer seemed quite so oppressive. It was no longer my sole focus. The relentless pressure was lifted, the skies cleared, and a shaft of sunlight shone through. So much so that for the first time since Louise died I felt the desire to remember the moment. This is the first positive new memory that I have made, the first hesitant entry in the blank journal of my new life. I found myself wanting to record the weekend, to capture and hold its spirit. I once more lost myself in taking photos, absorbed in the moment, and looked for souvenirs, including that mug, to mark the occasion for posterity.

That this liberation should happen at all was a surprise. But the fact that it occurred just days after the ordeal of Louise's inquest, a botched process seemingly designed to cause maximum pain to those who loved her, was quite extraordinary. The strange course of widowhood struck me again and again. If I had been able to clear my stunned mind for a moment back on that darkest of January evenings, what would I have thought had I known that it would lead directly to my presence here, in a Belgian bar in the early hours of the morning in the company of a group of widows and widowers?

There is a price to pay for the happiness and it is, inevitably, in guilt. Guilt that I should be enjoying myself when Louise is no longer here and incomprehension that just ten months after finding her body I can obtain this release.

There is bitterness too. I have this second chance, the opportunity to re-start my life, but Louise doesn't. Not for the first time I wonder why it was her and not me, why the fates decided that the less-deserving of the two of us should survive and be able to go on and enjoy moments like these. Louise was younger than me, more gifted than me, physically healthier than me. She was able, by virtue of her profession, to offer the world more than me and had a much wider spread of family and friends to feel the pain of her loss.

The return home was filled with apprehension. Acutely conscious that the moment was over and the contrast with reality would be stark, I stood in front of the empty and darkened house just as I had done the night that Louise died, dreading the loneliness and the inevitable tears that I expected to overwhelm me once I stepped inside.

And there *were* tears. But a week later, the almost euphoric afterglow, shared with so many others who made the same trip, is not quite dimmed. In one sense, nothing has changed. Louise is still dead, I am still alone. Yet this journey can surely never be quite as bad, quite as hopeless, again.

The pain of Louise's loss will not shrink and nor would I want it to. But for the first time I can begin to see how life can grow around it to the point that it is no longer all-consuming and it no longer defines me. I am crying again. But this time the tears are of relief because now I know that it is possible to get through this and live once more. Others have promised me that this will happen but I have now experienced it for myself. I have tasted good and will do so again. Happiness is attainable. Opportunity genuinely exists. Suddenly I can glimpse other signs of positivity and hope. I really am going to get through this.

As I opened the front door on Sunday evening, waiting for me in the post was a parcel containing the joining instructions for a holiday I am treating myself to, a once-in-a-lifetime trip that I am increasingly excited about. More new memories wait to be created.

Me, the Widower

20th December | 331 days

I may try and deny it. I may still wear a wedding ring. My Facebook profile may still declare that I am married. I may still invariably use the terms 'we' and 'ours' rather than 'I' and 'mine'. But I am a widower.

I am a widower. No matter how many times I use the term it still doesn't register. It's almost as if I don't hear my own voice. I can no more identify with such an unlikely description of myself than I can absorb the notion that Louise is dead. It's such a strange and alien label, one that carries so many connotations of age and decrepitude. Possibly the only widower that I knew well before now was my Grandfather and although he was actually only a little older than I am now when my Grandmother died, in my childhood recollection of him he was, probably rather unfairly, always frail and elderly. How can I be that person? Right here, now, in my mid-forties?

Maybe it doesn't help that the widower is generally a less visible figure in society than the widow. In part that's probably because there are fewer of us. Statistically speaking, it's the man who is the more likely to die young. We suffer from higher rates of heart disease, are reckless enough to be involved in more accidents and, ironically, are overwhelmingly more likely to take our lives.

It's also the case that we receive less media attention. It's not just that most of the human interest stories around bereavement focus on widows. This is probably inevitable given that those kinds of features tend to be of most interest to women and are therefore largely the preserve of media outlets speaking to a female audience. It's no coincidence that most literature on grief is written by and marketed to women. There is even a certain positive public image of a young widow: sassy, confident, defiant, ready to party and enjoy life. Widows wear stilettos. There is no obvious widower parallel.

But there is also the fact that women who have lost their partners tend to be more readily identified by their widowed status than men. A woman who has been bereaved in this way is very likely to be described in a news feature as a widow even if it is of no immediate relevance. A man much less so. Sadly, I suspect that this is at least partly because women are still defined more by their relationship to their husband, in an almost feudalistic possessive sense, whereas men have a status in society independent of their marital position. Even the language is revealing. Whereas, generally, it is the male form of a noun that predominates – 'actor' over 'actress' for example – the term widow is so all-pervasive that it's frequently applied to men as well as women.

The statistics also tell us that widowers are more likely to remarry than widows, and to do so more quickly. We remain widowers of course. The condition isn't cured by re-marriage any more than a lost limb can be re-grown. But superficially we are identified by our new coupled state, the loss no longer so readily observable.

And if the media tend not to talk about us much, it's also true that we don't much talk about ourselves. Even allowing for our numerical disadvantage there are relatively few men active within the young widowed community. This can easily be explained by the traditional tendency of men to grieve differently from women, to be less ready to express our emotions, to acknowledge the position we find ourselves in, to reach out and seek help. If we don't feel able to ask for directions when we are lost in an unfamiliar town, we are unlikely to ask for support or guidance when we have lost our emotional bearings in the maze of bereavement.

Even if we have the confidence – or the desperation – to try to do so, we often find ourselves prisoners of societal constraints. Real men are strong and silent, real men don't cry. Our male-orientated support networks of friends and colleagues are more likely to be focused on practical support, doing rather than talking, and it may not always be easy to express our distress within them.

Of course, not all men respond in an emotionally-closed way or lack the opportunity to unburden themselves to receptive friends, just as not all women want to open themselves up to such emotional engagement or feel able to do so. But the stereotypes exist for a reason and the one approach is recognisably broadly male and the other broadly female. And it's self-reinforcing. The more feminised the community of the widowed becomes, the more difficult it is for men to identify with it and sit comfortably within it.

This can lead to an isolating experience even for those of us who are instinctively emotionally open. The lack of male role models, either within support groups or the wider society, restricts the opportunities to 'learn' how to be a widower, to deal with the loss of our wife on both a practical and emotional level, and to see hope in the positive examples of those further down the path. I respond in my heart to the stories and struggles of widows because I can identify so readily with their emotions and experiences, but it's when I come across another man who has lost his wife and who plainly loves her and misses her, in the same way that I do Louise, that I am most moved.

The gender isolation is compounded when suicide is the cause of our partner's death. Fewer than one-in-five people who die by suicide are women so there are relatively few widowers who share the same experience as me. Despite frenetic networking with others who have lost their partners over the course of recent months I have met only one other man whose wife ended her own life.

Societal assumptions about our capabilities and needs as widowers also differ from those of widows. People tend to assume, admittedly with some justification, that without my wife I am helpless about the house and offer assistance accordingly. But they don't do so in respect of some of the more practical tasks which are more commonly associated with the husband. Yet it was Louise, not me, who possessed a sound sense of direction, basic DIY skills, and the ability to erect flat pack furniture. I came to rely on this and struggle without her but wouldn't feel able to call on anybody to help with a dripping tap or a blocked drain. It's just not done.

And then there is the wasteland of physical contact. I had a life full of hugs and cuddles ripped away from me without notice. One moment I was secure in the reassurance, warmth and comfort this offered, the next entirely without it, and at a time in my life when I needed it more than any other. I long for human touch, ravenous for a simple hug in which I can lose myself. Yet, as a man, this is particularly problematic. Platonic displays of physical affection towards a woman are liable to misinterpretation and towards a man almost entirely socially unacceptable in a way that does not apply between women. My hunger cannot be fed.

None of this is to suggest that the widower carries a greater burden than the widow. We share the commonalities of grief including the loneliness, exhaustion, bewilderment and guilt, even if our responses to them can sometimes differ.

And there are respects in which cultural expectations work in favour of widowers too. Men who seek another relationship relatively soon after loss, for example, tend to be looked upon more kindly than women following the same path. We have more permission to work off the anger that lies within everybody cheated by the premature death of their partner, and more outlets in which to do so. And perhaps the greater reluctance of society to define us by our state of bereavement, the readiness to see us as a whole individual rather than the broken half of a former couple, can sometimes allow us to escape the confines of grief more easily, to breathe the recuperative fresh air of normality at an earlier stage.

Perhaps it's as well that I struggle to perceive of myself as a widower. Acceptance of the label risks acceptance of the condition of grief, ownership of it not just for the short term but the long haul as well. To an extent this is inevitable. I am a widower and will always grieve for Louise.

But I do not want the rest of my life to be defined by this single fact. For I am many other things too. A son, a brother, an uncle, a public sector professional, a Brentford supporter, a history buff. And, of course, I will always remain Louise's husband. I prefer to be known for this, and to celebrate the fact that Louise lived, rather than exist for ever more in the shadow of the sadness that she died.

Last Christmas

26th December | 337 days

The words still ring in my ears, hollow and tragically ironic, twelve months later: 'There will be plenty of other Christmases for us to share'.

Louise was trying to convince me to leave her at home on Christmas Day in order that I could have dinner with my Mother. Though her mood was lifting rapidly after months of acute depression and anxiety she was not yet feeling strong enough to socialise. Torn, but fearful that it might be the last opportunity to share Christmas with my Mother after her serious illness earlier in the year, I reluctantly left for the afternoon without Louise. As it transpired I was right to be concerned that it might become a poignantly significant day, one to be forever remembered as an end point. I just chose the wrong person to spend it with.

I am nearly through the firsts. Birthdays, anniversaries, significant occasions, annual events, everything that the calendar can throw at me. The first time each will have been experienced without Louise. Each dreaded in advance for the emotional impact but each tending to be worse in the anticipation than the reality. Christmas is almost the last of these and one of the most challenging. A time to turn to family, a milestone by which the passage of time is marked and past holiday seasons remembered, and a time when the prevailing mood is, at least superficially, joyful and celebratory.

But my closest family is gone, remembrance is deeply painful and I am in no mood for celebration. Always previously my favourite time of year, enjoyed with childlike excitement, I approached this first Christmas without Louise on the assumption that it would hold nothing for me, dreading the whole season from the first appearance of Slade on the radio to the last of the leftover turkey.

My coping strategy was simple: avoidance. I kept the festive season at arm's length for as long as possible, the Christmas traditions that Louise and I were taking such delight in establishing together completely abandoned. No decorations went up in the house and my disinclination to watch TV protected me from the media frenzy. Cards were read but piled into a corner – other than the well-meaning but thoughtless one addressed jointly to my mother and I which was angrily and tearfully ripped up. It seems that in the eyes of some, widowhood has demoted me to the status of a child once more, again an appendage of my mother at the age of 47.

I have sought distraction too, opting to work right through to Christmas Eve, and will shortly leave for the biggest holiday of my life, booked partly to divert my focus from the time of year.

I managed to protect myself from the build-up sufficiently well to be almost surprised to discover that Christmas was finally upon me, yet inevitably there were still difficult moments, sometimes in ways which I hadn't anticipated. It transpired that I could hear the familiar Christmas music and put up with the excited chatter and bonhomie all around me without breaking down, even if I couldn't connect with the good cheer myself.

But reading sorrowful words about Louise's death in countless circular summaries of the year contained within friends' cards (and curiously never redacted for my eyes) has shocked over and over again, reminding me of the immensity of the loss I have experienced. If it's been the defining moment of the year for friends, I find myself grasping to try to understand just how much more enormous it is for me. Sometimes I need to see the reaction of others to pierce my self-protective layers of numbness and realise afresh how extraordinary, shocking and sad my own position is. It's curious how I so often see and define my own misery substantially in the reflection of the wider world.

And the one aspect of Christmas it was important to preserve, the buying of presents and writing of cards, has only served to further emphasise Louise's absence. I'm driven to honour and maintain her friendships in order to try to keep part of her essence close to me. But the presents and cards were previously Louise's domain. The fact that the tasks now fall to me is a stark reminder of my reality.

And it left me feeling inadequate, painfully aware of just how incapable I am of filling Louise's void as I struggled to decide on presents for people whose tastes I don't know, clumsily and painstakingly battled with the wrapping paper, and wrote cards to people so unfamiliar that I found myself constantly referring to our wedding guest list for Christian names to flesh out the initials and surnames on envelope labels.

Then there was the need to find a way of suitably honouring Louise, to begin the process of establishing new Christmas traditions, not of the celebration of the season but of memorial. A charitable donation in her name in lieu of a present, just as for her birthday, was easy but the Christmas morning visit to the park where her ashes were scattered much less so.

This was another of the countless occasions during the course of the last 11 months when I have been left struggling to absorb the enormity of what I've found myself doing as a consequence of Louise's death. When it has felt so implausible, so unreal, so bewildering that I have almost floated through the moment disconnected from my reality… observing myself and my circumstances as a bystander might.

Twelve months earlier, just before I departed for my mother's, Louise and I had enjoyed what transpired to be perhaps our last truly happy moments together, walking our dog around the same park on a bright, crisp Christmas morning. Louise had turned a corner, her depression and anxiety lifting. The darkness and struggle of the previous months seemed to be behind us. We chatted animatedly and examined the discrete memorial benches and trees, reading the inscriptions and wondering whether it would be appropriate to arrange something similar for Louise's father.

And now here I was, entering the park on another Christmas morning, moving self-consciously amongst the dog walkers as I clutched a bouquet of flowers, imagining everybody regarding with pity the man clearly come to mourn a lost loved one. I struggled to understand how last year's conventional dog walk had turned into this strange new ritual; Louise's death still not owned by me in any remotely meaningful way. How did I get from there to here?

When I returned to the park the following day, however, I discovered a passer-by had moved the flowers to a better position than I had thought to leave them in, securing the bouquet more firmly against the wind. A small gesture of kindness which filled me with gratitude. Not for the first time over the holiday my spirits were lifted. Of course there have been tears, and naturally my mind has continually wandered back to what we used to do at this time of year, and what we should have been doing now. How could it be anything other when I turn in bed on Christmas morning to wish my wife a Merry Christmas but to speak only to pillows and an empty space?

But against all expectations there have also been moments of enjoyment and I found myself yielding to the traditions of the season more and more, determined not to allow Louise's death to entirely steal away the opportunity for precious family moments and new memories. It's been a busy time, filled with people and activity. Perhaps sometimes almost too much, since I missed the space to continue to grieve in the private ways that I have become accustomed to over the year. Louise's family, as well as my own, have held me close, just as she asked them to in her farewell letter.

Grasping for consolation, I tell myself that in a sense Louise was right after all. She may not be physically present but her spirit continues to live within me and I carry both her and her memory forward. This connection, and the continuing love of her family and friends, enables me to feel that on one level at least, I was still able to share Christmas with her and will continue to be able to do so in the future.

It hasn't been the Christmas that I wanted, of course, nor can it possibly ever be again. But once more I try to remember that although I constantly compare my broken present with my perfect past it is pointless to do so. I do not have the luxury of choosing between what I used to have and what I have now. My choice is, instead, between passively accepting that diminished present or doing all I can to make it as good as it can possibly be. And in those terms, over this holiday at least, I succeeded.

The Cape of Fluctuating Hope

29th December | 340 days

I always try hard to find a positive perspective on this journey. It's completely contrary to type. My outlook on life is naturally pessimistic. But I decided quite early on that hope was the only thing that I could rely upon to guide me safely to the end of it, to bring me out of the desert.

At first it was enough to merely have hope that there would be hope. But it's now forming itself into something more solid and attainable. I have reached a point where I no longer always need to force myself to actively seek out that hope. It can sometimes come to me quite spontaneously. The road is markedly easier to navigate.

However, I have also realised that while the terrain may change it is, in some respects, a journey without end. I will never fully escape from the desert. I am currently in Cape Town, on a holiday ostensibly to watch cricket but primarily designed so that I can be in the country of Louise's birth on the last day of the last year of her life. It's a major achievement for me. I have never done a long-haul trip before and as a nervous flyer found the prospect of another kind of journey – the flight – daunting. And of course I haven't travelled anywhere without the comforting presence of Louise by my side for several years.

Nevertheless, I've been looking forward to the holiday for a long time. I started planning it just a couple of months after Louise died and, as time has gone by, have become increasingly excited not only by the prospect of everything that I will see and do on the trip but also by the validation that it will bring: a sense of renewal and accomplishment, a step forwards in the direction of 'normal' life. I've been quietly quite proud of myself.

That is, at least until tonight when the respective tectonic plates of hope and reality have violently crashed together on the first evening. Sitting in a restaurant having dinner it suddenly struck me that it was the first time I have eaten like this on my own since everything changed. When the waiter asked me 'Are you alone?' and promptly removed the other place settings to leave me sitting in isolation, I nearly lost it. He wasn't to know that his question, and my response, spoke to something far bigger than whether anybody else was joining me for dinner this evening.

Neither was he to know that I had been feeling lost all afternoon, ever since I had emerged from the hotel to explore my new surroundings for the first time. My limitations without Louise were cruelly exposed. Where once we would have enjoyed a textured and comfortable experience on holiday, now I wandered aimlessly, uncertain of where I was going without Louise's sense of direction and without either the courage or the motivation to do the simple things that slow down and enrich travelling: stopping at cafes and bars for drinks to linger and enjoy the view, buying treats from stalls, interacting with locals, searching out a good restaurant. I was always too shy to do that myself and, besides, without Louise with whom to share the moment what's the point?

So I just carry on walking, only scratching the surface of the experience, just as I used to before meeting her. But the difference is that now I know that there is better. I had it and lost it again.

And nor could the waiter have known that I was already beginning to understand the myriad other ways in which holidaying alone would accentuate Louise's absence. The lack of somebody to share the moment with, to talk about what had been seen and done, to reflect on it and to register it in a collective memory so that the experience could be remembered and refreshed in the years to come. The lack of a different perspective on the location, one which would introduce me to sights and activities that I wouldn't otherwise try, and the lack of somebody to photograph and be photographed by.

I loved taking beautiful pictures of Louise almost more than anything else and now here I was visiting breathtaking locations, planning in my mind the photos that I would want to have taken of her and at the same time regretting that there would now be none of me to mark my visit. I hadn't appreciated when packing how essential a piece of equipment the selfie stick is for widowers.

Perhaps most significantly though, I was already acutely feeling my separation from others in the tour group. As I looked around me at the welcome drinks session I noticed that almost everybody else was part of a couple, something that I hadn't anticipated beforehand. This wouldn't previously have been a problem. Couples interact with couples. Louise and I would have found a niche. But on my own I was the odd one out. I resorted to pretending to take a close interest in my phone to try and explain why I was standing completely alone. I wasn't sad and single. I had merely received an important text message.

I suddenly realised that there was a chasm of experience between my fellow travellers and myself. I wanted to be part of their comfortable, domesticated world but I can't be, not now, maybe not ever again. I can't be not just because I am now one where before I was two, but also because my innocence and complacency have been shattered. I can't be because my wife put a dog's lead around her neck and kicked away the stool that she was standing on. This was what can only be described as a 'What the fuck?' moment of realisation. I was grateful to be able to delay the breakdown until I was safely back in the privacy of my room.

I had thought that I could do this. I have been away several times in my new life as a widower already. But on each occasion this was with either family or other young widows and widowers, people who knew about what had happened and understood what it meant. I had underestimated the challenge of re-entering the big wide world beyond. I've come all the way to South Africa to find Louise yet she seems further away from me than ever before, her absence almost more noticeable than in the new routine which I have begun to create and accept at home.

But then what else am I to do? Never go on holiday again? Avoid all non-widowed couples? Tempting though it is to retreat back into my shrunken comfort zone, that would do nothing to help me grow the rest of my life again, to ensure it surrounds and absorbs the impact of Louise's death. I'm tired and emotional, battered by the shock of my first real day of holiday on my own. I have barely slept in the last 36 hours as I was unable to do so on the overnight flight. Some kind of reaction was almost inevitable. There are lots of exciting activities to look forward to in the coming days.

And I shouldn't make assumptions about the life experiences of the other members of my tour party. It may be that those around me who seem so distant, so privileged, have their own stories to tell. It may be that they embody the hope and normalisation that I long for so much.

That pesky positivity will reassert itself. Appropriately, tomorrow I visit the Cape of Good Hope, a place so named because of the optimism it encouraged in 15th century sailors due to the opening of a new route to India and the East, a means of easing a long and treacherous journey. The parallel in terms of my own hopeful path seems clear.

For Auld Lang Syne

3rd January | 345 days

The beat of the music from open air concerts on the trendy Waterfront district was interrupted by fireworks soaring into the air against the awe-inspiring backdrop of Table Mountain and the drunken cheers of the sweltering crowds of locals and tourists densely thronging the streets and packing the quayside bars and restaurants. Cape Town was celebrating the arrival of the New Year with a carnival vibe and I found myself wondering whether or not to join everybody in welcoming it in or to regret the passing of the old year.

Louise and I never marked New Year. We preferred to spend the evening quietly at home and were often in bed before midnight. But soon after her death I decided that it was important for me to be in the country of her birth on the last day of the last calendar year of her life. I was never entirely clear why. Louise was born to a British family and remembered virtually nothing of her early years in South Africa. The family connections with the African continent remained strong, however, and there was some nebulous sense of closing a loop, honouring her by bringing both ends of her existence together.

And having travelled 6,000 miles for the occasion, it seemed as though I should do more than sit in my hotel with a room service sandwich and quietly reflect and write. So, as midnight approached, I joined the crowds and counted down the final minutes of 2015. It was another surreal moment on this strange journey which has led me to the most unlikely of people, places, activities and achievements.

Rationally, the New Year should have no particular significance. It's just a date. Just the start of another of the 340 or so days since Louise's death. But the symbolism is strong. While it might sound strange to want to hold on to a year which has brought so much misery, the worst of my life by a countless multiple, I can't help feeling as though the passing of the old year takes Louise further out of reach, placing her, for the first time, very firmly in the past.

I can no longer talk about what we were doing together this year. Since Louise died in January, I can barely talk about what we were doing together last year either. Our last really precious memories and times together, our last holidays, our last Christmas, the last shows and family events we attended together, are now back in the apparently distant past of the year before last.

I can no longer even say that my wife died 'earlier this year'. This is important because of the sense of remoteness it engenders. I worry that people hearing the story for the first time will fail to understand the continuing impact of it, assuming that at such a distance I must be 'over it'. And I worry that those who already know the story will begin to forget. To forget about Louise and, as the firsts turn into seconds, to forget about me. When you have lost your partner in a world designed for couples you forever fret about becoming invisible.

It also feels like a step away from Louise because she didn't know this New Year. It's part of an ongoing process which will steadily leave her behind. Things that will, over time, become familiar to me; people, events, fashions, technology, will never be familiar to her. It will become more and more difficult for me to talk to Louise without having to explain background and context. Just as she will forever remain 40 while I continue to age, she will always remain in 2015.

This divergence in experience and knowledge started the moment that Louise died and has continued with each day that passes, from major life events – she never knew our niece, born three months after she took her life, nor the baby daughter of one of her best friends – to mundane domestic rearrangement and refurbishment. She doesn't know that the temperamental dishwasher has now been replaced, the gift from a Guinean Olympic delegate who stayed with us during the London Games has finally been framed, or that we have a new TV and broadband connection. Somehow the arrival of a new year accelerates this process. We are connected by the past and separated by the future.

But while the distance from Louise that 2016 signifies is distressing, I welcome the fact that it also offers distance from the act itself, the days around it and the most acute stages of grief. Not a fresh start exactly, but a chance to clear my head and begin to try to live life again. I'm proud that I have at least survived to reach this point, a landmark that was so distant eleven months ago that I could barely even conceive of it. In some respects, contradictorily, the fact that people may treat me as a normal robust human again rather than a bereaved object of sympathy and pity is also good news. The coming year may bring less of the angled head and sympathetic eyes. I might still need to wrap myself in the cloak of widowhood much of the time but more and more frequently it feels liberating to discard it.

The reason that Louise and I didn't celebrate New Year was because of the sense of uncertainty and foreboding associated with an unknown future. Last year, ironically, we agreed that for once this was absent. The previous twelve months had been so traumatic both for us and our respective families that we were grateful to escape into a year which we were convinced could only be better.

Perhaps it's foolish to tempt fate in the same way again. However, I have to believe that the coming twelve months will be more positive, a time when I am able to continue to honour and remember Louise but can also make space for other things and allow my eternally busy mind some respite. A time too when hope begins to be converted into something of substance as I lay the foundations for my new life. And a time, dare I say it, when I end a year happier than I begin it.

Risking Love Again

18th January | 360 days

There was one line in Louise's farewell letter which cut even deeper than the rest. One line which never failed to leave me howling in pain long after daily reading and re-reading of the contents had drawn the very worst of the shock and hurt from the remainder. 'I so much hope that in time you will meet a loving woman who will be able to give you the life you deserve.' In her confusion of the moment, Louise had managed to convince herself that somehow I would be able to lead a better life without her, that somebody else could give me more than she was capable of. Never can anybody have been more tragically mistaken.

I spent half a lifetime looking for Louise. Shy, socially awkward and blessed with anything but film star looks or a stand out personality, dating never came easily to me and brought precious little success. I always remained convinced, however, that I would eventually be rewarded for my perseverance, for the countless excruciating evenings meeting women from the online dating sites and the accumulated wearying, confidence-sapping weight of numerous rejections and humiliations. One day, I knew, I would meet somebody very special who would make it all worthwhile.

And when I did, she was more than anything I had ever dared dream of, somebody who fulfilled needs I hadn't even previously realised existed. Perhaps it was because we met relatively late in life and the search had been so long, but familiarity never dulled my appreciation of my good fortune. Every day of our lives together I gave thanks for the remarkable privilege of being Louise's husband. Each time that I saw an advert for a dating website I heaved a sigh of relief that I would never have to look for 'the one' again. I already had her.

But now she is gone. And things would be much more simple if I could be pure and true, content to dedicate the rest of my life to Louise's memory. But of course I'm weak, lonely and just plain human and desperately want to try and recreate something of what I once had. I yearn for all those things a stable, loving relationship provides which were ripped away from me in an instant; companionship, human touch, a sense of oneness, something that fills the void in my heart and my home. And above all I want to love and be loved, not just in the abstract realm in which my relationship with Louise is now forced to exist but in the tangible reality of the day-to-day experience.

Almost from the very beginning of this journey I have therefore held on to the hope that I will one day find love again. I've used this hope as motivation throughout the long and difficult year, the ultimate destination in my mental road map of the route to recovery.

I am not yet ready to reach that destination. There is no right way to approach new relationships after bereavement other than our own. No minimum sentence of loneliness must be served for the sake of propriety. But I have always been clear in my mind that I wanted nothing in the first year, partly to allow me to properly remember Louise and partly to prevent the risk of hasty decisions in the vulnerability of the moment. At present, all I require is simple companionship. But I can sense that the time is nearing when I need more. When I need once again to love.

I have Louise's permission, almost an instruction, to find that love. I owe it to her to seek it. To spend the rest of my life in noble but lonely isolation would make her sacrifice even more wasteful, even more tragic, than it already is. I am confident that there is no contradiction between continuing to love and honour Louise and holding similar feelings towards another woman. Love is not a finite resource. A parent loves a second child no less than the first and so it would be with another wife.

Nevertheless, the prospect of dating and loving again hurts, scares and confuses me as much as it consoles and excites. It is probably the most complex of all the issues which I have to grapple with in the establishment of my new life because it most directly challenges all my notions of love and commitment to Louise which have sustained me thus far. Despite Louise's encouragement, despite the knowledge that the need to think about such things was not of my choosing and despite the ability to justify my need and my right to seek another relationship, it is still difficult to avoid a sense of betrayal merely in the contemplation of it.

I gained a sense of how deep-seated this emotional response was, and how far I would have to travel to overcome it, in the relatively early days. I found myself unable to tolerate a friend of more than 20 years standing making a cup of tea in my kitchen. In our kitchen. In Louise's kitchen. The presence of another woman where I was used to seeing Louise, even in the most innocent of circumstances, jarred painfully.

I have progressed since then, shocking myself to the core on the first occasion after Louise's death that I realised I felt an attraction to another woman. But the fundamental challenge remains. How do I let another woman into my life without feeling that I am cheating on Louise? How do I touch, kiss, enjoy intimacy with somebody who is not Louise? I would never have dreamed of doing so in other circumstances. How do I overcome the barriers of emotional conditioning that four-and-a-half years of love and assumptions of lifetime exclusivity build? Louise and I told each other we were One and would be so For Ever. What do those statements mean if I meet somebody else? And what do I say to them in turn?

Overlaid on this confusion is fear. Fear of the difference between a new partner and Louise and the disappointment this will bring. My much used phrase of 'finding love again' is a gentle euphemism which hides the challenging reality that it really means being with Somebody Else. Somebody who is not Louise. Somebody who will think, act and treat me differently. We will do different things, respond to each other in different ways, live different lives.

This is difficult to come to terms with when my idea of what a relationship looks and feels like is defined by the one Louise and I enjoyed. It's too easy to fall into the trap of seeing re-marriage as a panacea, something which will give me back exactly what I had and sweep away the pain. This is chasing an illusion. It will do neither.

It is imperative that I fully understand that my relationship with Louise is gone and I can never have it back, that I understand and accept at every level of consciousness that another relationship will be very different. Otherwise I will be forever unfairly and unfavourably comparing my new partner with Louise, allowing no opportunity for the relationship to establish itself on its own terms. I need to be able to appreciate being with somebody for who they are and not for who I want them to be. I need to understand that the choice is not between Louise and another woman but another woman and nobody.

There is fear too that a new relationship might not just be merely different... it might be inferior. Before I met Louise I would have been prepared to settle for something 'good enough', but having now known much better than that, 'good enough' is no longer sufficient. The bar is set extraordinarily high because anything less would make a mockery of what Louise did and what she hoped for me.

And opening myself up to love again exposes myself to another risk, that of further loss. The death of my partner is, for me, no longer a theoretical abstract possibility, something which most people of my age can safely push to the back of their mind as a comfortingly far distant and impossibly un-knowable experience. It's something which I know intimately, something which I am acutely aware can occur at any time. All things being equal, there would be even odds that at some point I would, once more, find myself the one left behind. How could I possibly put myself in a position where I might experience this pain again? I've picked myself up from the floor once but doubt that I have sufficient strength to do it a second time.

But maybe I am worrying unnecessarily. Because even if I find the strength within myself to accept these risks, even if I decide to tolerate the humiliation of initially having merely the casual status of a date or a boyfriend, and even if I prepare myself to start the exhausting task of building another relationship from scratch, beginning the long haul of getting to know somebody else as intimately as I knew Louise, I may never be given the opportunity. This is not merely because of my own inadequacies but because, in the eyes of many, I have too much 'baggage'. As a widower, it seems that I am, at best, suspect, and at worst to be avoided entirely.

I discovered this harsh truth as soon as I tentatively started to search online for inspirational examples of widowers finding new loves. Dating a widower was clearly a staple topic of agony columns, invariably based upon the potential lack of commitment to a new relationship from a widower who is perceived to have failed to 'move on' from his love for his late wife, as evidenced by some crime of sentimentality such as the continuing presence in his home of photographs of her. The advice is often to steer clear of those with split loyalties, those who still demonstrate the merest flicker of memory and love for the woman who was their whole life.

It seems to me bizarre that people expect those who have lost partners to quietly forget about them. The societal expectation that once we lose the person closest to us in the world we should seek to replace them and then deny the memory of them is unique to the loss of a partner. We don't expect bereaved parents to take down photos of their children, or siblings never to talk of their deceased brothers or sisters, so why should widows and widowers? Why should the display of love for your partner, which in other circumstances would be viewed as the right and honourable thing to do, suddenly become undesirable if you are seeking to build a new life after loss?

The widespread suspicion of the widower (or widow) as partner is, in any case, counter-intuitive. Widowers have demonstrated that we know how to love, to sustain a relationship. Our marriages worked. They did not end in the divorce courts. If we have been so badly hurt by grief but still want to experience another relationship, to open ourselves up to all those risks once more, if we are prepared to overcome all the challenges, doubts and guilt that dating will bring, we must be truly committed to the idea of love. We, above all others, know the proper value of it and will cherish and nurture it where we find it.

Perhaps it's not surprising, then, that I can currently only conceive of a relationship with a widow, somebody who shares the same experience of loss, somebody who understands. In my idealised imagination, an imagination which nurtures the hope that sustains me, we balance each other, both of us bringing two people into the relationship; ourselves and our late partners. We celebrate and honour each other's memories and marriages. There are three sets of wedding photos on the walls.

Of course life, and love, rarely follow the expected course. Maybe I would find it easier simply to accept that the confusion and guilt will melt away when I meet the right person, widowed or otherwise. Rather than being simply a theoretical notion as it is now, the reality of love will ensure that things fall into place naturally. And while I know that some women will be unable to cope with the past that I bring with me, they are not the ones that I seek in any case.

Just as I always had hope that I would meet an amazing woman who would become my wife, now I have hope that one day I will meet another extraordinary, clever, gentle and wise woman. A woman who recognises that I am still, and always will be, Louise's husband, and who allows me to hold and honour that, but who also understands that there is no contradiction in the same heart belonging simultaneously to two wives. Not split in half, but wholly given to both. And when I do, she will be the woman that I know Louise wants for me.

The Longest Year

23rd January | 365 days

My Sweetheart, it's now exactly a year since the fog swirling around in your mind became so dense that it obscured all hope, a year since you took what you saw as the only practical solution open to you in order to ease the pain.

It's a year since we cuddled up to each other in bed, a year since I heard you tell me that you love me, a year since I saw your smile, felt your touch or shared your presence. It's a year since I last read to you, made you your favourite cup of mint tea, or massaged away the tensions of your day. It's been the longest year of my life, one in which I have hurt over you more than I ever thought it was possible to hurt, cried over you more than I ever thought it was possible to cry, and loved you more than I ever thought it was possible to love.

It's a year which I never thought would end, a horizon which, at first, I couldn't even imagine, much less see. As I lay on my sister's sofa covered in blankets, shivering with shock and willing that first interminable sleepless night of widowhood away, I was able to think only in terms of surviving minutes. Gradually, as time passed this became hours, days and then weeks until, eventually, I knew a significant victory had been won; I had stopped counting the weeks and started counting the months. At every small landmark on the way, at first every Friday, then in time every 23rd of the month, I found myself surprised, and a little proud, to have reached that point, both relieved to have put distance between myself and that hideous evening but deeply sad at the distance that was also emerging between us.

I still worry about you endlessly; whether and what you are thinking, feeling, experiencing. I struggle to comprehend your reality now. I wasn't with you when you died but I have been able to piece together most of your last day, what you did and said and, by extension, what you felt. I imagine, over and over, the sight of your last moments, though curiously it is only in the last few days that it has occurred to me to wonder about the *sound* of that struggle. Every time that I stand outside the front of the house and prepare to enter it, or look out of the window, particularly in the dark, I remember those moments this night a year ago, beyond chilling, beyond words, when I stood locked outside the house knowing that you were inside, dead. Every time that I walk through the hallway I picture you as I found you.

I have done things during this long year which I never imagined I would have to do and would not wish on my worst enemy. In the early weeks, particularly, each day seemed to bring a new previously undreamed of horror; walking through the door of the undertakers to arrange your funeral, sitting alone in a candlelit room saying goodbye to the waxy half-likeness that purported to be you and summoning up the courage to kiss your now cold and hard lips for the final time, trying to find the words for my eulogy, having to announce your death over and over to dozens of call centres as I dealt with the endless bureaucracy. Even the day that I paid off our mortgage was one of the saddest of my life.

I am exhausted. Grieving is a full-time occupation. It consumes all my emotional energy and saps my physical reserves of strength through sleeplessness and the restless, incessant drive to memorialise you, to honour you and to preserve your memory. Almost everything that I do is connected in some way to the events of twelve months ago. I look back far more than I look forward. My concentration span is shot to pieces. I am still unable to contribute at work in quite the same way as I was before, operating at only three-quarters capacity. I find it difficult to motivate myself to do anything which is not connected to you. Getting out of bed is the hardest part of the day.

And then there is the loneliness as I struggle to adapt to living alone for the first time in my life; the silence and stillness around the house, the cold and empty side of the bed next to me, the empty chair at the dinner table. The lack of anybody to discuss my day with, to share experiences with, the absence of human touch. The lack of your comforting presence by my side when I wake in the early hours after a nightmare and realise that the reality is worse than the dream.

It's a cruel irony that it is precisely because you have gone that I need you more than ever. Perhaps the very lowest point of all came when I stood at the Crematorium in the freezing cold of a February morning watching the hearse slowly pull towards us. Turning and glancing at those family members gathered behind me, I dimly registered that – almost without exception – all were huddling into the arms of their partners for comfort. But I stood alone, exposed. You were unable to offer that same support. *You* were lying in the coffin being borne towards me.

I know that to those who have not experienced a loss such as this it will sound as if I am not coping, not 'moving on'. I have received much advice over this year, all of it well-intentioned, much of it wise but some of it hurtful in its simplistic ignorance of the complexity of the emotions of grief. I smile politely and refrain from asking how somebody who has not experienced this most shattering and unique of losses can presume to know what I should be doing and how I should be feeling.

But please do not worry about me Louise. There is no need. If I have learned anything during this year it is the remarkable power of human resilience. It is almost as if my brain has shut part of itself down in order to protect me from the worst aspects of the shock and trauma. The whole experience has seemed so bewildering, so unreal, that I can barely relate to it as my own. I still cannot grasp the simple fact that you have died and I have been widowed. At the very worst moments, I have floated through almost as if it were an out-of-body experience, present but not feeling, observing rather than participating. It makes it possible to survive what would otherwise be unendurable.

I take great pride in the fact that I have got through without a major breakdown. I still function, still go to work, still meet my other family caring responsibilities. I still watch Brentford every week and, to my surprise, find that the outcome genuinely matters to me. Despite the memories of this night a year ago, I am still at least tolerably relaxed in the home that we built together, able to take comfort from your association with it and the sense of continuity and normality.

I have been holed but have not sunk. It is the greatest achievement of my life. I have emerged from the year with a new self-confidence, a sense that if I can deal with this I can deal with anything.

And there have been other achievements beyond mere survival. Bereavement has led me to some strange places. In the course of the year, I have been inspired to do things that I would previously have thought beyond me, that I would never have had the courage or the initiative to do were it not for my burning need to honour you and to look after myself in a manner which I hope you approve of. I have set up a charity, become a blogger, written a book, travelled further than I have ever done before, spoken at a medical conference, fulfilled our promise to investigate Quakerism, and participated in and established networks of suicide survivors.

And I know that you will be most surprised of all to learn that I have cast aside my natural shyness to wholeheartedly plunge into a whole new social world. Some friends have fallen by the wayside, perhaps those who did not know how to reach out to me, or who were afraid to do so. I have not had the time or the energy to take the initiative on their behalf.

But other friendships, some of them unlikely, have grown out of the generous support offered to me. I am honoured to be even closer to many of your friends, and your family, than I was before, enabling me, in a sense, to continue to represent you. And I have joined a whole new social network of fellow widows and widowers, emboldened by the thought that you would wholeheartedly approve.

So, I have now finally reached the long-anticipated anniversary, a date redolent with meaning and symbolism. I have found myself becoming increasingly distracted over the past week and more tearful than for some months. Much thought went in to deciding how best to mark the occasion – not just the anniversary itself but yesterday too, the equivalent day of the week, the day when the rhythms most closely matched those of your last. It was important to be where I should have been the evening that you died – at home. A candle from our last holiday together, in Sicily, flickers as I reflect and write.

That reflection enables me to understand that the anniversary effectively marks two quite different things. It is clearly about endings; your life, our time together. It is a moment to look back on what has gone, to remember you and recall with deep sadness the agony of your last moments, moments which I am replaying in my mind minute-by-minute as the day wears on, building to the very eye of your storm. The day marks one year of life that you have lost, of things that you have missed out on. And for me, one year of separation from you. It is a figure which will grow inexorably. I hold on desperately to the hope that you are now so happy that you have not missed that year, but I do not have the certainty of faith to properly reassure me.

But the anniversary also marks a beginning; a year since the start of my subsequent journey through life without you. The symbolism is strong. Whilst it too is a story of sadness, it is one which allows the possibility of recovery and re-growth.

There is a sense of triumph over adversity simply to have reached this point. I often use the metaphor of a journey because it feels very much like a transition from one place of being to another. But perhaps this feels more like successfully scaling a mountain. I can't help believing that now the shape of my grief will change, that I will give myself more permission to move forward. That does not mean forgetting you, or letting go of my love for you. Nor even does it mean that I will stop mourning your loss. But perhaps I will now feel able to begin to grow the rest of my life around that loss, allow myself to smile, relax and enjoy myself without guilt, to lift my head and look forward as well as back.

I'm aware of the dangers of investing too much hope in the landmark. So much focus is placed on completing the first year that it's easy to forget that nothing substantive will magically change. When I wake up tomorrow morning you will not have returned. I will merely be faced with the reality of the grind of starting the second year of the long journey without you. I know that this can be a difficult time in itself.

I am, however, extremely glad that I am now here rather than where I was this time last year. The very worst is over and I have got through it. If, on that

Friday evening twelve months ago, I had been able to look forward to this point today I would have been largely relieved at what I saw. My life is infinitely poorer and sadder than it was with you. I have travelled a difficult path and there is further, much further, to go. I will, in fact, never stop walking it until the day that I join you once more. But despite the occasional detour into difficult terrain, the path gets easier to follow and sometimes, unexpectedly, grants me a wonderful blessing en route.

I would never have chosen this direction for myself but having been given it I have found that it makes it easier to endure if I accept it, attempt to understand it, and put my trust in the hope that I will eventually be able to find happiness once more. At least I know now what I didn't when I stood twelve months ago, just a few feet from where I write this now, and looked into your open but unseeing eyes; it is a journey that I can and will survive. And I am doing it as much for you as I am myself. My Sweetheart Louise, my best friend, my hero, my hope, my inspiration, my beautiful wife; I miss you so much. I love you so much.

CPSIA information can be obtained
at www.ICGtesting.com
Printed in the USA
LVHW020955010419
612522LV00005B/577